Brampton Library

ABOVE THE NOISE

ABOVE THE NOISE

My Story of Chasing Calm

DeMar DeRozan

WITH DAVE ZARUM

Collins

Above the Noise
Copyright © 2024 by DeMar DeRozan, Inc.
All rights reserved.

Published by Collins, an imprint of HarperCollins Publishers Ltd

First Canadian edition

No part of this book may be used or reproduced in any manner whatsoever without written permission.

Without limiting the author's and publisher's exclusive rights, any unauthorized use of this publication to train generative artificial intelligence (AI) technologies is expressly prohibited.

HarperCollins books may be purchased for educational, business, or sales promotional use through our Special Markets Department.

HarperCollins Publishers Ltd
Bay Adelaide Centre, East Tower
22 Adelaide Street West, 41st Floor
Toronto, Ontario, Canada
M5H 4E3

www.harpercollins.ca

Library and Archives Canada Cataloguing in Publication information is available on request

ISBN 978-1-4434-6988-3

Book design by Jo Anne Metsch

Printed and bound in the United States of America
24 25 26 27 28   LBC   5 4 3 2 1

*To my father, Frank DeRozan,
the man who made me who I am*

"This depression get the best of me . . ."
February 17, 2018. 3:06 A.M.

FOREWORD

Coach Gregg Popovich

I became personally involved with DeMar when we traded for him and brought him to the San Antonio Spurs in 2018. He was devastated at the time for a variety of reasons, and upon his arrival it was obvious to me he was in need of a safe space to believe the world could be just and fair once again. His story is one of adaptability, courage, and love—just ask his family, especially his children, who are truly his passion.

DeMar DeRozan spent his young days trying to be a kid, avoiding danger and carefully existing in Compton, California. This young boy was experiencing his world with an innocence that belied reality and soon morphed into a realization that danger abounds everywhere, and survival became an all-consuming effort. Most of us have no idea how that world shapes a perspective on life and what harm it can do over time.

Amidst the influences present—many of which are not conducive to a life of order, safety, and success—one learns that the childhood world of simple play and joy may just be a myth that needs adjustment and a heavy dose of reality. DeMar came to the conclusion that finding an inner circle of people with whom he could confide, depend upon, and love was the prudent path to achieving some safety and peace.

He witnessed too much of what no one would wish for anyone, but he figured out the decisions and choices that had to be made to help escape what many could not. In this regard, certain family members, mentors, and coaches helped him navigate his path. Without them, he very likely could have ended up like others in hopeless situations—incarcerated or dead.

This story of persistent effort on his part to rise above is compelling and important, for it was not without a price. As DeMar found basketball and understood the vehicle it could be for an escape, he bore down and became an NBA star. His life experiences remained, of course, and his thoughts of how he could have achieved so much in spite of the chaos and dangers would linger. The pressure to stay the course, as so many he knew were unable to do, and meet the expectations of others was a constant mental strain. He knew very well that many depended upon him, both fairly and unfairly. He was quite brave in openly speaking about what would be a topic too often avoided—depression. His was and is real, a condition mostly hidden, especially by people in the public eye. We now know what a problem this is for millions of people across the nation, and his willingness to be transparent speaks volumes about his character, which exudes a love that is tangible for all to see.

He has actively pursued an understanding of this malady and endured with grace and success in a world of debilitating expectations. DeMar has been able to maintain relationships with family members, teammates, coaches, and friends who support him, and he has given them in return empathy, calm, and love. His improbable success in dealing with his past and present will be tested once again when he decides to leave the court and pursue the next chapter in his life.

PRELUDE

I pull up to the parking lot of Lueders Park Community Center in Compton with my dad, who's wearing my jersey (the nameplate on the back proudly reads "DeRozan Dad"), and my first-born daughter, Diar, who's four years old at the time. It's 2017, and I recently wrapped up my eighth NBA season with the Toronto Raptors and third as an all-star. I'm back for a ceremony to name the indoor court at the rec center the "DeMar DeRozan Gymnasium"—a huge honor and a chance to spend some time with kids in the community. As badly as I wanted to better my situation, I've always been fiercely loyal to the place that raised me. To give back and be an example for the kids back home meant the world to me. It was bigger than basketball.

Lueders Park is a couple miles northwest of where I grew up. It famously has an outdoor swimming pool surrounded by a barbed-wire fence so people can't sneak in, and a large playground out front. I used to play in a basketball league there once a week during the summers when I was a kid, but outside of that I had been taught to avoid Lueders Park. That was Blood territory.

After the ceremony wraps, I chat with a group of kids who've attended the free basketball camps I hold in Compton each summer. I always come back home so the kids can see me and know that they can achieve their dreams—whether it's in sports, school, medicine, whatever they want. I do a couple of interviews with the local media, and then head outside with Diar, who is begging me to play around on the jungle gym outside. She approaches the yellow plastic slide. "Look, Daddy!" she says excitedly, pointing to a maze of graffiti covering the slide, gangs marking their territory. "Somebody colored on the slide with a crayon!" I'm struck by her innocence and so grateful at that moment. I think about how much I'd been exposed to when I was young—and how protected my daughter is from it all. She has no idea what she's looking at. When I was four, I knew *exactly* what that "coloring" was.

The city I grew up in was so territorial. One uncle, who lived near me, was a Crip who was killed by a Blood. Another uncle, who lived in a different part of town, was a Blood killed by a Crip. That's how it went. The street gangs were everywhere. The Bloods and Crips were the biggest—notorious rivals, each with dozens of crews, divided by geography—but there were also large numbers of Hispanic and other gangs, too. It had been that way since the seventies. Over the next two decades, Compton found itself in the middle of America's crack epidemic. The gangs' numbers grew while the city suffered. I remember once reading a statistic about how there were something like forty-five different Crip gangs in L.A. in the seventies and more than two hundred now, with more than seventeen thousand members in this city alone. Same story with the Bloods.

Where I was raised, damn near the whole neighborhood was Crips, including some of my best friends and closest family members. Growing up, it was all I knew. Even though I was never in the gangs, they were everywhere around me, which meant that I was raised in an environment where death and destruction were normalized.

From that early age, I would see constant reminders, like seeing somebody get shot in broad daylight. People being shot over a simple miscommunication. I'll never forget one night when I was six or seven looking outside my front window and seeing a dead body lying in the street outside my house. The kind of thing no child should be seeing. The body stayed there, in a heap by the side of the road, for hours until a wagon finally came to pick it up. I'd hear sirens and helicopters at all hours, and at night I'd watch the floodlights from the choppers lighting up the entire block like some sort of UFO up in the sky. The sound of gunshots was as everyday as the sight of the sun. It was such a part of our daily lives that you don't even react. You'd hear that distinct, unforgiving sound of a bullet leaving the chamber and you'd just shrug, *Here we go again.* The sounds always came in a sequence. First the gunshot, then you'd hear the burning rubber of a car squealing off, drowning out the shouts and screams. I mean, you can do the math . . .

I couldn't explain why things were the way they were. I couldn't explain why people I loved were dying around me and why my parents and I attended funerals as often as other families went to the movies. I couldn't explain why I could meet up with some of my cousins in person, but others I could only speak with on the phone from their jail cells, and I'd have to wait years to see them up close again. I couldn't explain why everybody had to act so goddamn tough all the time and why it seemed like danger lurked around damn near every corner. All of it made me angry. It made me so mad to watch my mom wiping away tears after another family member was killed. And I carried the burning around with me everywhere I went. I'd lie awake at night—I guess you'd call it insomnia—my mind running full-court sprints. I knew I needed to talk about this feeling I carried with me: the anger, and a heaviness. But I didn't know how. So there it stayed, bottled, shaken. Ready to explode.

That anger became my motivation—to run faster, jump higher, stay in the gym an hour longer no matter how tired I was. Basketball became how I handled it. Sometimes it felt like that was all I needed. More often, it still wasn't enough.

It wasn't easy trying to be a kid in a place where making it through each day alive felt like an accomplishment. Today, I wear my upbringing like a badge of honor. The city, harsh as it was, is what made me. If it hadn't been for everything I learned growing up in Compton, I wouldn't be the person I am today. But back then? It made me angry.

PART ONE

CHAPTER 1

I'm my mother's only child. The doctors told her they didn't think she could get pregnant or have a safe birth. It's why she always called me "The Blessed One." The rest of my family—cousins, aunts, uncles—called me that because I was one of the few kids fortunate enough to have what it takes to make it out of my environment. I was born on August 7, 1989, in Compton, California. My mom named me "DeMar" after her brother Lemar, who was shot and killed when he was twenty.

Diane Dykes, my mom, was born and raised in Compton. She's a tough woman—you'd have to be the way she was raised—who lives with lupus, an immune-system disease that causes severe joint pain. It's been that way since I was young. But she doesn't let it hold her down. Mom used to work manual labor jobs when I was a kid. She worked at a factory assembling thermostats until I was ten. That's when she got into an accident when a machine landed on her leg. It was real bad and she had to get screws put into her foot.

Mom's family is really big. She has six siblings—and everybody was close. Growing up I was surrounded by her family. Cousins, aunties, uncles, grandparents. They were my whole universe. Mom has a twin sister, Donna, who was like a second mother to me. The two of them were staples in the neighborhood. Everybody loved and respected my mom. As I got older and she wanted to shield me more and more from the gang scene that dominated the Compton streets, the whole community knew to respect her wishes. I think part of that was because of the respect and admiration my uncles received. Two of my mom's brothers were high-ranking gang members. Uncle Kevin, like most everyone I grew up with, was a member of the Crips. The other, Uncle Lemar, was in the Bloods. (Technically he was her half-brother and lived with my grandfather in a different part of the city.) Where I grew up, it seemed like everybody had ties to one gang or another.

My dad, Frank, was from a small town in Louisiana called Vidalia. With the exception of the poverty, Vidalia is as different—and rural—as you can get. Dad was Old Country through and through. Hardworking. Unforgiving. Never complained. People called him Big Dog. He was large, tall, and imposing; he knew how to occupy space. Big Dog was a football player—a middle linebacker—and all-around athlete in his younger days. Matter of fact, Dad was the first Black player on the Vidalia High School basketball team. In his first game, he grabbed thirty-six rebounds. After playing college football at Grambling State in Louisiana, he did what everybody did: headed west to California looking for a better living. He settled in Compton, not far from the block where my mom lived.

Dad had two kids from a previous marriage. My sister, Vanessa, is fifteen years older than me, and my older brother, Jermaine, was seventeen when I was born. My half-siblings lived in a different house with their mom. It wasn't far from us, about five miles north in Lynwood, but I never had much of a relationship with either of them until we were all older. It was hard to find common ground when I was a kid. They just grew up so differently—their lives seemed calm. Besides, the age difference between my half-siblings and me was massive: By the time I could walk they were already out of high school.

Mom and Dad met at the Compton Fashion Center, aka the Swap Meet, a Compton landmark that has since been shuttered, like so many hangouts from my days. The Swap Meet was a massive indoor flea market where you could go to find all manner of knock-off clothes, counterfeit sneakers, and fake diamonds and jewelry. It was where my friends and I would pick up a pair of fake Air Jordans and catch the latest fashion trends, the whole time dreaming that one day we would be able to own the real deal. My mom used to always tell the same story of how they met. She was shopping in a shoe store when my dad spotted her through a throng of people from outside. He approached her, working up the courage to ask for her phone number.

"Boy, you're going to have to buy me these shoes if you even want to *think* about getting my number," she told him. Mom wasn't kidding. So, he bought the shoes. The two were practically inseparable from that moment on.

Mom's family accepted my dad with open arms. He wasn't loud and didn't need to be front and center, but he was a guy who naturally commanded respect. Mom's dad, my grandfather, Otis Dykes, coached youth football in the community and began coaching alongside my dad in the local Pop Warner league. Mom never let me play football, even though it was one of the most popular sports in Compton. Practically every kid in the neighborhood grew up playing football. (Dad and Grandpa coached the rapper Eazy-E when he was a kid, which always blew my mind.) Once, my mom and dad went to see my brother Jermaine play in a high school game. In the fourth quarter, he was knocked out cold by a vicious tackle. That was all Mom had to see to know her own son was never going to meet the same fate. She wouldn't let me near the gridiron. Instead, my first sport was something a bit more safe: tee-ball.

◦ ◦ ◦

I grew up in a ten-block area occupied by the Corner Poccet Crips. Damn near the whole neighborhood was part of the gang, including some of my best friends and closest family members. The territory you lived in was protected by whichever gang ran that block, and even if you're not in the gangs, you still lived by their unwritten rules. That meant knowing to mind your own business, understanding the consequences of wearing a certain item of clothing, or learning which blocks were safe and which weren't. If you saw someone you didn't know, you had to get more information.

"Where you from? Where you stay? Where yo' mama stay? Where yo' daddy stay? What school you went to?" That was pretty much all you needed to know to tell if someone was or wasn't a threat. In Compton you were a product of your environment, whether you chose to be or not. You came to learn which are the Crip streets and which are the Blood streets, where the Hispanic gangs hold territory, and what areas you needed to avoid if you didn't want trouble.

Our house was a four-room townhome on Acacia Court. Outside, there was graffiti everywhere you looked—not those beautiful, colorful wall murals by street artists like you'd see in other parts of Los Angeles. In Compton, the graffiti was a way for gangs to mark their turf. There was a dead tree leaning on the house beside ours, and a trash can that was always kicked over at the nearest street corner, garbage strewn about. The city never bothered to come by to fasten the can to the sidewalk, or to help clean up the mess. They didn't care. Nobody outside our hood cared how we lived. That's how we felt, at least.

Our house backed onto the Gardena Freeway and had a wrought-iron fence around the spotty patch of grass we called a front yard. All of the houses were separated from the street with an iron fence, but it's not like it made us feel any safer. Walking through the front door, you entered into the kitchen. We didn't have any furniture except for two beds—one for my parents and one for me. (That didn't change until I was twelve and we moved to a furnished house up the block on a street named Myrrh, in the heart of Original Poccet Hood Crip territory.) There was an old TV in my room that sat balanced on top of a dresser, with two silver antennas poking out the back. It didn't matter which way you moved them, I could never get anything but that static snowstorm on the screen. On top of the TV was an even older big-ass VCR that I used all the time, sitting on the edge of the bed watching videos all night. I still remember how that machine would swallow up the tape cassette. The click of the machine and the sound of tape running through the reel was so loud it practically drowned out whatever I was watching. In the kitchen, we used an ice cooler instead of a refrigerator. Mom or Dad would send me on trips to the corner store to buy a new block of ice once the old one had melted.

Not that I had much of a clue, but we were seriously down on hard times. There were signs everywhere you looked. The sink never worked in the bathroom, so you had to turn on the bath spout to get water to brush your teeth. But the water never ran long enough to be able to fill the tub and take a bath—only enough for a fast shower, or a sponge bath. At night I'd hear rats running inside the walls. That house left me forever humbled.

But at the time? I didn't think twice about it. Our neighbors lived the same way as us. We all shared in the same struggles. It all seemed very normal to me. I didn't think nothing of nothing. Still, I could figure out that my family was fighting to barely scrape by. There were nights where we weren't sure what we were going to be able to eat. As a kid I never really liked school, but it got to the point where I would look forward to going for the sheer fact that I knew I would be provided with a free lunch. So I'd be guaranteed at least one meal that day.

We had nothing, but I never resented my parents for our situation. I could see how hard they worked to provide a roof over our heads. That's all I could ever have asked of them. There were so many nights I spent home alone, probably way too young to be on my own like that, but my parents had to earn a living.

For a while, my dad worked at the Compton Cable Company, delivering and installing cable boxes to homes throughout the city. Then he found a job working in video production for the city of Compton. He would be down at City Hall, standing behind the camera filming council meetings or programming commercials for the local public-access TV channel. He was always into TV and movies. Maybe it's why he chose to settle in Los Angeles. One of the biggest perks of his job was that he had access to one of those dual-tape VHS machines that allowed you to make duplicates of any videotape. He would record stuff off of the TV at his work (we never had cable at home) onto a blank VHS tape. Or he would rent a movie from the video store, place it into one slot, insert another blank tape into the other, and make a copy of the video to take home. It wasn't long before the walls of our furniture-less living room was stacked floor to ceiling with videotapes.

Dad was working all the time. He'd leave early in the morning and wouldn't come back until late. So many weeknights I tried to wait up for him for a chance to see him before I went to bed, fighting my eyes from shutting for the night. More often than not, I failed. I'd fall in and out of sleep in my bedroom and wake up the next morning to the sound of crisp toast popping out of the toaster or eggs sizzling on the burner. I'd walk into the kitchen to my dad fixing me breakfast, which he did each morning at 7:15 like clockwork, shirt neatly tucked into his khaki pants, fully dressed and ready to head out to work after my meal was cooked. I came to really appreciate the times on the weekends where we could just hang. I looked up to my dad. He was larger than life.

○　○　○

The hot Pontiac had been bumping along the interstate for nearly ten hours. We were headed east, to Vidalia, Louisiana, to visit my dad's side of the family. Twenty-seven hours of driving each way. We made the trip, Mom, Dad, and me, every summer until I was around thirteen. I stared out the window as the landscapes slowly changed. The concrete streets of Compton turned into endless grids of California farmland, which morphed into a desert backdrop, the sun setting while we passed through Arizona toward the New Mexico border, roughly the halfway point.

Before we got to the hotel, Dad pulled the car over along the side of the I-10.

"Look up there, DeMar," he said, competing with the chirp of the crickets somewhere out of sight. "You can see the stars from here."

He pointed up into the sky. I looked up at the map of stars lighting the night sky. It was the most amazing thing I'd ever seen.

"Why don't we ever see no stars in the sky where we live?" I asked.

We *never* saw the stars back home. In Compton, Dad explained, the L.A. lights were the only thing that lit up the sky in the dead of night. And that, where we lived, the light pollution from street lamps and highway lights behind our house made sure you never forgot you were in the city. Just like how, when all was quiet at night, you could still always hear the steady hum of thousands of cars rolling up and down the freeway.

"You see that bright one up there, D?"

I squinted. "I think so?"

"That's the North Star."

I stared up at the sky and pointed up toward the moon, which seemed to be glowing.

"OK, let's get back on the road. Time to go," he said, motioning us back inside the car. I asked if we could stay longer and he shook his head. Before he dropped himself into his seat he paused, placing his hands on the frame of the driver's door, looking over the roof to me on the other side. "You know the great thing about the moon?"

"No, what?"

"You may not always be able to see it but, just like the stars, the moon will shine again tomorrow. Now get yo ass in the car."

We never saw the stars back in Compton, but on some nights you could still see the moon. I was entranced by it. To me, the moon represented what was out there beyond where I lived: an entire universe. When you come from a place like Compton, where outsiders are afraid to enter and most people don't have the means—or imagination—to leave, you're raised in an insular world. All everyone knew was Compton. But I always knew there was more. And as much as I loved the people I grew up with and was loyal to the city that raised me, I needed the hope that the night sky provided. By the time I was a teenager, when my city was becoming more and more of a war zone, knowing there was more than this world kept me focused on my goals in basketball and using hoops to lift us out of that environment. So many nights I would drive to Manhattan Beach, or to the beaches of Santa Monica, alone, find a quiet spot, and just stare at the moon.

The stars were even more incredible once we arrived in Vidalia. I swear you could see *Every. Single. One.* Dad saw how taken I was with it all.

"Just wait until I teach you about the constellations," he cracked.

Being a city kid, the adjustment to Louisiana was wild. That country shit was night-and-day different than anything I was used to. Man, it was another world. Mosquitoes everywhere. Roaches the size of my thumb. No sidewalks. My dad's family came from little means and lived in the same house he'd grown up in. It felt like walking into a time machine. To heat water you had to fill a pot and place it on a wood-fired stove. To flush the toilet, you had to pull on a little chain hanging from the wall. I thought we had nothing, but it made me appreciate that no matter where you stand, there's always going to be someone who has less.

I remember my dad took me out to cotton fields where he used to work when he was younger. Long hours in the sticky, blazing sun, lucky to take home just a few dollars for his effort. He showed me how the cotton grew out of a bulb like a flower, and demonstrated how it was picked. I didn't even know cotton grew like that.

Each time I came home from those trips I gained more of an understanding of my dad. I began to see why he would work so damn hard even if there was never much of anything to show from it. I learned why he didn't have room for any excuses. I learned why, years later on the basketball court, he would constantly push me to my limits—and to the point of tears. It was the only way he knew how. Same was true for everyone in that town. Sunup to sundown. Nothing glamorous. He had grown up worshiping the virtues of hard work and was damn well going to make sure I did the same. Where Pops was from, everybody worked their ass off—and for basically nothing. But to them it was everything.

I grew a deeper appreciation for my mom and dad and what they did for our family. I feel like I can face anything thanks to them, like my problems now are minor in the grand scheme of things. After all, where we grew up it was an accomplishment just to make it through each day.

°   °   °

As hard as my parents worked, it wasn't a pretty scene at our house. We never used to invite people over—because of the living situation we just couldn't. I guess that's why I was always at Grandma's house, which acted as our family headquarters. Grandma lived about ten minutes from us, in a house painted green like the color of money. She had a small front porch we used to hang out on all the time and a short white fence around her front lawn that never quite stood up straight. It was always leaning over. In front of the house was a loquat tree we used to pick the fruit off of to eat. Beside it was a thorny tree that grew roses, and beside the rose tree was another tree that, whenever I or my cousins got into trouble, we had to tear a branch off and pick all the leaves off the branch. That made it into a switch, and Grandma would give us whoopings with it. It was soft and flexible, and it hurt like hell.

With seven kids of her own, Grandma had tons of grandchildren, and my cousins were the heart of my social circle growing up. Come to think of it, that's still true today. Whenever I was at Grandma's my cousins seemed to be there, too. We'd play all day—it was like you had no choice but to be outside. My elementary school was two hundred yards from Grandma's house, and it had an asphalt basketball court behind a locked gate that my cousins and I would use after school, or during the weekends. We'd hop the metal gates, mindful of the sharp top on each fencepost, and play until the school police arrived and kicked us out. Then we'd go back to Grandma's and attach a milk crate to a lamppost or a dead tree, and use that for a basket.

My cousins and I did everything together. And they're the exact same dudes now as when we were younger. We used to get in fights with each other, but if anyone tried to mess with us, we always protected one another. They've always been my support group. If it weren't for my cousins I might not be here today.

My eldest cousin is MC, the son of Auntie Donna, Mom's twin. He's always been the overseer of us all, watching our backs and making sure we stayed out of trouble, even if he couldn't always do the same. When I was a little kid, MC was sent to jail. He went in when he was just sixteen and stayed locked up for a little over ten years. The entire time he was in the joint, we would speak on the phone. Every two days. No matter what.

"You're working hard now, right?" he'd say. "Make sure you don't give your mama a hard time. And remember you gotta look after Grandma until I'm back."

"Yeah, and when's that?"

"Soon, D. Soon."

To me there was nothing unusual about those calls. Everybody in the neighborhood had family members in jail. My calls with MC felt like the most normal thing in my life. Just chatting with my big cousin.

My cousin DeShaun is the jokester of the group, always keeping things light and making us laugh—we all shoot jokes all day whenever we see each other (I like to say we get together to play, just like when we were kids)—but DeShaun is definitely the main culprit and the one I've probably spent the most time with. My cousin T—Trunnell—is another big kid in the group. I grew up watching him play basketball. Looking back, he was all right, nothing special, but I swear when I was younger I was convinced T was a future hoops star. James, who is the more serious type, was most similar in age to me—I think he's a year younger—and I remember having sleepovers on the floor of his room. And then there was Kevin, who lived at Grandma's house and, outside of my half-brother Jermaine, felt like the closest thing I had to a brother.

I had so many cousins—too many to name—but those are the ones I've remained closest to.

I'm just about the youngest one of the group, so I always looked up to them in some type of way. Some, like MC, felt more like uncles than cousins. Together we've all experienced the fucked-up cycle of growing up in Compton in those days. Guns. Gangs. Death. Destruction. One of the reasons I've stayed so close to them is because there aren't many people who are a positive influence on me who've been through the things we've been through together.

Maybe it's because I was "The Blessed One," but for whatever reason I was always Grandma's favorite grandchild. She had this big cookie jar that sat on her kitchen counter and she would always wait until I was there before she filled it up, to make sure that I got a cookie. My cousins used to get jealous and it led to fights at times. But that never seemed to stop Grandma. There'd be so many times when me and my cousins would all be chilling at her house. We'd hear the ice cream truck go by, circus music blaring from speakers and bouncing across the asphalt until it reached our ears. "DeMar!" she'd call out. "Come over here and take this dollar and go get yourself a treat."

Before basketball, Grandma was my peace. She was the calm element in my life. Even when there was chaos all around me. Like so many surrounding me, I was an angry kid, a product of my environment. At school I would get in trouble a lot for fighting. My dad would have to discipline me often, putting me in my room for timeouts. If I'd really laid a whooping on somebody, or if I was talking back to him too much, he'd lock me in our broom closet. To Grandma, on the other hand, I could do no wrong.

I used to always make these grand promises to her. Even when I was a little kid, when the thought of making it to the NBA wasn't even on my radar, I used to wrap my arms around her and tell her that I was going to take care of her family, make sure her grandkids were looked after. She would smile—"Come here, sweetness"—and give me a hug.

When it came time to leave Grandma's house I would throw a fit. I loved being with my cousins, and I loved being around Grandma. I loved how comfortable everything felt at her place. I was with my closest people, there was cable TV, a nice couch, a spare bed for me to sleep in, and always cookies in the jar. I was so happy there. I didn't want to go home. When my dad would come to pick me up I would cry and wail and beg to stay longer.

"*Boy*," he'd say, unimpressed by my performance, his voice tired from a long day's work. "*Get yo ass in the car.*"

CHAPTER 2

I was always hoopin'. It was just how we passed the time in those days. But it wasn't until I started watching old games on TV with my dad that I became truly obsessed, unlocking a fascination that, to this day, has never faded.

Dad and I used to sit on the floor of our living room and watch videotapes of decade-old NBA games. You know that grainy eighties footage, where you could barely make out who was who and the arena lights would leave bright streaks across the screen? I couldn't get enough of it. Dad and his friends would trade tapes, and he'd use the dual VCR recorder at work to make copies and bring them home for me. I was transfixed by the players on the screen and the way they moved, like superhumans capable of walking on air, pulling off every move in the book. Hell, they were *writing* the book. I'd watch old tapes of Julius Erving—Dr. J—one of the godfathers of hangtime, leaping off the hardwood and soaring to the rim, his white-and-blue Philadelphia 76ers jersey ruffling in midair like feathers. I'd watch Alex English, the Denver Nuggets star who could score from anywhere on the court and had an arsenal of moves that seemed never-ending. (Soon after I began my career in the NBA with the Toronto Raptors, the team hired English as an assistant coach, which was so crazy to me.) I'd watch George Gervin when he was on the Chicago Bulls, and Dad would explain to me how Gervin was past his prime by then, and how, in his younger days with the San Antonio Spurs, he was the coldest dude on the court—it's why they called him the Iceman.

Pretty much any sport I tried I was good from the jump. Baseball, track, soccer, you name it—I was just an athlete from day one. But they were always treated as normal activities, you know, something kids do to pass the time. When it came to basketball, however, I was completely locked in from the age of four. Dad could see that, and took it upon himself to give me a thorough education in the game. And I couldn't get enough of it.

By the time I was eight or nine, the stacks of VHS tapes filled our living room, lining each wall from floor to ceiling. Each one was carefully labeled. Dad would write the date of the game, the teams playing, and would usually add something notable on the cassette—"MJ 69," for example, on the tape of Michael Jordan's career-high scoring night in 1986.

The tapes weren't *all* NBA footage. Dad was a movie buff, an interest he definitely passed along to me. Because we didn't have cable TV growing up, the videotapes were our nightly entertainment. I couldn't wait until the weekends, because that's when Dad and I would rent movies from the local video store. We had a whole system: On Friday we'd rent a pile of movies. At some point on Saturday, Dad would make copies of them, and we would return the tapes to the store early Sunday morning so we didn't get charged the full weekend rental rate. We would watch all kinds of movies, from *The Godfather* to *Toy Story* and everything in between. To this day I'm a movie fanatic. Life in the NBA means being on the road so often and spending a lot of time in planes and hotel rooms, so I think a lot of players end up watching more movies than your average person, although from what I see, the younger players in the league these days are only interested in video games—sometimes more than basketball. Dad was always showing me a lot of older movies, especially old-school blaxploitation films and any movie that starred Jim Brown. Yes, *that* Jim Brown.

But nothing felt as special as watching those basketball tapes. We'd stand in front of the piles and make a selection for the night, and then class was in session. We would pause the games every few minutes to talk about what we were watching. "Why did he pass the ball like that?" I'd ask after seeing Magic Johnson whip the ball behind his back into the waiting hands of James Worthy, somehow catching his teammate in stride. Dad would explain that he did it to trick the defender, who couldn't track where the ball was going. "But wait," I'd say. "*How* did he pass the ball like that?"

The "Showtime" Lakers teams of the eighties was always a go-to for Dad and me. By the time I was born, that Lakers dynasty was on its last legs, but in the days before we had internet, our tapes kept the team's legacy alive in our household. One of my favorite tapes to watch was the iconic Game 4 of the 1987 Finals between the Lakers and rival Boston Celtics. I can still see it in my mind: With the Lakers down by one point in the dying seconds, Magic Johnson has the ball in the left corner. The Celtics forward Kevin McHale comes out near the three-point line as Kareem Abdul-Jabbar posts up and calls for the ball. Magic doesn't pass it. Instead, he loses McHale with a step-back dribble and signature head fake. He takes off toward the free-throw line. Three white Boston jerseys swarm him the moment he gets there, but Magic takes off and winds his right arm up toward the sky, uncorking a hook shot that falls perfectly through the mesh with two seconds to go. The Lakers win, 107–106, and would go on to capture the title two games later.

I knew from watching countless tapes that the skyhook was Kareem's signature move. So when I saw Magic pull the shot out of his arsenal to win the game for the Lakers a spark went off in my head. *Oh, so he learned that move from his teammate.*

"Wasn't that the skyhook, Dad? That's what Kareem do, right?"

"Exactly, D," Dad said, proud as can be. He'd tell me the whole story of how Magic would emulate Kareem, rehearsing the skyhook in practice, but never used it in a game until that very moment. "It's a shame more players don't use the skyhook more, but, fact is, it's way harder than it looks; you got to be so damn good to be able to pull off a hook shot like that." Each VHS tape was like another piece of a puzzle toward understanding the game—how players developed moves, how those moves all had various counter-moves, and how adjustments were constantly being made as the sport evolves. Those connections with basketball sparked a deeper connection between me and the Big Dog.

In the morning, after Dad made me breakfast, I'd beg him or Mom to take me to the nearest court, at Wilson Park off Alameda Street, before school so I could try to replicate what I saw on tape the night before. As I started to take basketball more seriously, I began to mimic the pros more and more and it felt like I was able to step inside their minds. Like I was one of them. I even got pretty good at hitting the skyhook. Then at night before bed, I'd re-create the opening scene in *Space Jam*, when a young Michael Jordan is playing imaginary hoops in his bedroom. Like Mike, I'd run through the short hallway separating my parents' room from mine, pretending I was taking off for a dunk. Then I'd bound into my room, plant my pivot foot, and shoot an imaginary fadeaway, sticking my tongue out like MJ as I fell back on the bed. *Swish.*

In 1998, when I was nine years old, I had my first brush with the NBA up close and personal. We were a Lakers family, and we'd go over to Grandma's to watch them play on Channel 9, KCAL, whenever we had the chance, damn near every game. I didn't watch too many Clippers games, but I knew who their point guard, Darrick Martin, was. In the late seventies, he went to high school nearby in Long Beach, where he was a McDonald's All American, and after that he starred at UCLA. Martin had some relatives who lived on my grandfather's street just a few doors down. He'd been friends with one of my uncles and got to know Grandpa over the years. One day, during an off-day in the NBA season, Martin came down to Compton to visit and wound up hanging out at my grandfather's house. When word got around that Martin was there, my cousins DeShaun, Kevin, James, and I rushed over as fast as we could. Martin was never a big star—he bounced around the league during a thirteen-year career before getting into coaching—but to us it might as well have been Michael Jordan standing in Grandpa's living room. When I arrived I could barely muster a word. An NBA player? In *Compton*? I just stared in disbelief. *Why are you here?* The thought ran through my mind on repeat. It was one thing for my dad to tell me I can make it—everybody's parents say stuff like that. But to see someone like Martin in the flesh like that made it feel real. He was breathing the same air as me. His skin looked the same. He was a regular human.

That day is a big reason why I make sure I return to Compton as much as I can to visit schools and be around the kids. If someone like Martin had that effect on me when I was young—to inspire me with his presence alone—then maybe seeing me can help give a kid the belief that they can do anything they want with their lives, whether it's becoming an athlete, a doctor, a pilot. Anything. I just want them to feel what I felt meeting Darrick Martin.

In a place like Compton visibility is everything. I'll never forget driving by Compton Park at Myrrh and Atlantic, Dad pointing out to me every time we passed it—"Look, DeMar!"— telling me that's where Venus and Serena Williams first practiced. Whether it was the Williams sisters dominating on the tennis court or guys like Dr. Dre, The Game, and Nipsey Hussle making a name for themselves in the rap game, just to know that it was possible to start in Compton and finish on top of the world meant everything. Visibility mattered. But my dream wasn't tennis. And it wasn't hip-hop. It was hoops. Seeing Martin that day was a real lightbulb moment for me. *So it IS possible,* I thought.

Before long, basketball was the only thing around me that I could comprehend. I never understood exactly why death rates in Compton were on the rise, and I couldn't grasp why someone would fire a gun to settle a dispute. I struggled to explain why Ma had lupus, and I didn't really know what it meant for MC to be in jail for more than a decade—how life-altering that must be. But I understood basketball, and I built my whole world around it. It was my identity. It was my outlet and my therapy. Basketball was my ticket out.

I knew my dad felt the same way. The truth is, he was always telling me that I could be something long before I ever realized it myself. It got to the point where he said it so much that I started to believe him. Today they'd call it "speaking it into existence," "manifestation," and all that. But I think he was just calling it like he saw it. I was physically mature from a young age. In grade school I was always the biggest kid. I was a natural athlete. I was coachable. And I loved to play. When I would hit a tough shot, or pull off a move that I'd been practicing in a game, I'd think, *Maybe he's right. If I did that, what else can I pull off?* That kept me going.

My dad saw a bright future for me. It must be why he pushed me so hard. Until high school, Dad was the central coaching figure in my life. And, man, he worked me. As a coach he was impossible to please. If I messed up, he let me know. If I did a good job, he'd tell me it don't matter unless I can do it again. "We're out here putting another stripe on the tiger today, ain't we son!?" he'd say when I complained.

I'm ten, eleven, twelve years old, and Dad would take me out to Wilson Park and put me through drills—shooting from different parts of the floor, dribbling up and down the court with either hand, crossovers, free throws—every day was a different focus. I loved having something to lock in on. Despite being so young, I knew kids that age—hell, friends of mine—who were already getting caught up in the traps of the neighborhood. They wanted to be just like the OGs on the block, hustling on the corners and getting into trouble. I wanted to be like Jordan, like Kobe, like Dr. J and all the other legends I watched on tape. Dad wanted that, too.

When it came time to play in organized games—local rec leagues, or on the school team—Dad was still on my ass (back in those days he never missed a game). If I let somebody score on me, he'd yell out "You let *that* motherfucker do that to you!?" It seemed that I could do no good in his eyes. I could pin the ball to the backboard with a nasty block on defense, send a picture-perfect outlet pass, sprint down the court and fill the lane, catch the ball on the run and slam that thing on some poor kid's head and get fouled in the process for an and-one. There'd be oohs and ahs from the other kids and parents in the stands. But if I missed the free throw, you would just hear Dad's voice booming through the gym. "Come *on!* You owe me five push-ups." When I'd get home, he'd make me follow through on my debts. We'd win the game by forty points and I'd be back home doing push-ups in my room for punishment. It made me so mad. Mom would always point out that the more angry I was, the better it seemed I played. It's something I'm still aware of today.

Dad and I would always be playing games of one-on-one. They would get so heated. It was like a scene in *He Got Game*, a movie we would watch together a lot, times a thousand. In the film, Denzel Washington portrays Jake Shuttlesworth, who tries to persuade his son, top prospect Jesus Shuttlesworth, played by NBA star Ray Allen, to attend a specific college. It culminates in an intense game of one-on-one. At first, Jake gets the better of Jesus and runs out to an early lead, until his son roars back and dominates his old man. It took me years until I could regularly get the best of Dad on the court.

He never took it easy on me. He'd block my shot so hard it would send me collapsing to the ground with the ball. "Get up," is all he'd offer, no hint of empathy. I would drive to the hoop and he'd dip his hefty shoulder into the small of my back so hard that my feet left the ground. The more he pushed me around, the angrier I got. Tears would pour down my face. "What? You soft? You think somebody else is going to take it easy on you?" he'd offer. "Nobody out here cares about your tears. Get up, crybaby." Half the time the games ended when I punted the ball into the streets.

And still, each day I went back to the court with him. I honestly couldn't wait for that shit. As I reflect on it all now, I can't help but think, *Why?* Why was I so excited to go back every day, knowing the emotional roller-coaster I was riding? The tears, the fights, the pain. Yeah, it felt good to see progress and know that I was getting better. But you know what it really came down to?

More than anything, I just wanted my dad to tell me I did a good job. For years, that was my biggest motivation in basketball.

In quiet moments, when the heat of our on-court battles wore off, he'd put his arm around me. "I'd rather be hard on you now," he'd tell me, "so once you go out into the real world you can handle it. Because they're not gonna have no love for you. Remember: Nobody out there has your back." By the time I was making a name for myself in the NBA, we'd reminisce about those training sessions. I'd call him after a particularly tough game. One night when I was playing for the Toronto Raptors we were in New York City for a game against Carmelo Anthony and the Knicks. We were down big for most of the game, but we made a huge comeback in the fourth quarter. I hit the game-winning shot—a fadeaway jumper, the kind I used to take in my bedroom as a kid before bed—with 1.9 seconds left. "See, that's why I wanted to teach you resilience," Dad said on the phone on the way to the airport. "I wanted you to be able to handle adversity, to play through your emotions and be able to use your mind even if all you see is red," he said. "You know, DeMar," his voice softened slightly. "One day I'm going to be gone and I won't be here for you, either."

I knew that my dad loved me, and to me he was larger than life. But he was also the only person I was scared of. And I was terrified. It got to the point where, truthfully, I was scared to have a son of my own. I knew I couldn't deliver that same brand of tough love and I didn't want to feel like I had to apply the same foundations as a father that my dad did to me.

I was intimidated by Dad, but the feeling wore off as I got older. By the time I was in high school and he had stepped back from my basketball development, he got to be a parent again and not a coach. And, as teenagers tend to do, I tested my limits with my parents. I stole my dad's Pontiac at night a couple of times. OK, maybe more than a couple. It went on for two years straight, during my junior and senior years. I would take the car and go see a girl, or meet up with my best friend, Davian, and hang out. Some nights, I would just drive to the beach by myself and stare at the moon.

I worked out the perfect operation: It didn't matter if my dad worked late or not, he was always fast asleep by 11 o'clock. Like clockwork. Around 10:30 or 10:45, when I heard his bedroom door shut for the night, I would go into the kitchen, where he always left his keys on the counter. I'd tiptoe into the room, grab the keys, head outside, and sit in the Pontiac, which was parked on the street in front of our home. By this point we had moved from our place on Acacia Court to a slightly better house on Myrrh Street. Behind the house was a Blue Line metro station and the train would zip past every fifteen minutes. I'd sit and wait until the moment the train passed until I put the key into the ignition and start the car, and the noise of the rail hydraulics and the train whistle would drown out the wheezing engine of the Pontiac. I'd shift into drive and head off for the night, then get back around two or three in the morning so I could at least get some sleep before my 7:00 A.M. wake-up call for school. It was flawless. Almost.

One night, I took the car a half-hour west to Manhattan Beach and got lost in the moon. By the time I returned home it was two in the morning. I got off the Gardena Freeway and made the left turn from Acacia Ave onto Myrrh. As I approached our house, I couldn't believe my eyes. There was another car parked in front in the exact spot where my dad had left his Pontiac. I was panicking. No clue what to do. So I sat in the car, hoping that the people would leave before Dad woke up at 7. An hour went by. Then three. I ended up sitting there on lookout until 6:45, when the car finally rolled out of the spot. I pulled right in and rushed inside before my parents were awake. I was sweating like it was the fourth quarter. That was the last time I ever took his car.

It wasn't until I was in the NBA that I had the courage to tell him that story. He couldn't believe it. "Man, I *knew* something was up!" he said. "For two years I thought the neighbors had been siphoning gas from my car!" It had never occurred to me to refill the gas tank after my night drives. No wonder he had been suspicious. If he knew back then, Big Dog would've wanted to whoop my ass. But he took it well. He couldn't stop laughing. It was the hardest we ever laughed together. "Hey, as long as you ain't ever get in trouble and never hurt nobody, it's cool."

                                    °   °   °

All the lessons with Dad were paying off. At school, I was regularly beating the older kids on the court. We weren't even on the same level, to be honest. I was growing—fast—over six feet tall by the seventh grade and I could leap with the best of them. I loved dunking on kids who were older than me. And believe me, the feeling was not mutual.

Ever since I was in middle school I've had the nickname "Deebo." It's what everybody back in Compton calls me, and it's a name that's followed me to the NBA, where most players I'm close to will call me "Deebo" and almost never "DeMar."

The character Deebo is the nemesis in the Ice Cube movie *Friday,* which takes place in South Central Los Angeles, near Compton. Deebo is taller than everyone, and he's tough, aggressive, intimidating, and always getting into fights. Naturally, everybody always assumes that I got the nickname from the character. They're wrong. In the climactic scene in the movie, Ice Cube's character, Craig, finally stands up to Deebo, the neighborhood bully, and beats him senseless. It's his hero moment. *That's* where the name came from.

One day in the sixth grade, I was in PE class playing basketball with kids from multiple grades. This dude from the eighth grade was guarding me. I was blocking every one of his shot attempts, and scoring any which way I wanted against him. He was just getting embarrassed in front of everybody. Near the end of the game, I backed him down in the paint, lowered my shoulder into him to create space, and lifted off the ground for an easy bank shot. He'd had enough and before the ball fell through the mesh, he shoved me hard into the basket post. I was raised to never let anyone push me around, so I swung at him in retaliation and a huge fight broke out between us. It wasn't pretty for him. He wasn't getting a piece of me and I was getting *all* of him. Eventually he stormed off and everybody on the playground was making fun of him. I almost felt bad. As he was walking away, my buddy Davian yelled out, "DeMar beat him up like Craig did to Deebo!" The name just stuck. Everybody called me Deebo from that moment on. Friends, teachers, everyone. For the longest time, if somebody called me Deebo, I knew they were from back home, that they were in the club, so to speak. I have no idea how the name followed me to the NBA. It's one of those things where an opponent would call me Deebo during a game and I'd think, *How the fuck do you even know about that?*

o o o

"Are you all right, Big Dog?" I asked my dad. He didn't answer. He was locked in on the road, hands fixed at ten and two on the steering wheel of the Pontiac. The drive from Compton to my brother Jermaine's house in Hollywood usually took about an hour, but we were taking it slower than usual. It was a Sunday, when Dad would sometimes take me over to visit Jermaine and play dominoes. I was twelve and Jermaine was twenty-seven. He had his own place, which was cool, and he coached a local AAU basketball team in Compton.

But something was off. The entire drive, the car kept swerving left.

"Hey, you sure you OK?"

Dad would steady the car in the lane and then, a few seconds later, we'd veer left again. Swerving and swerving the entire trip. I unbuckled my seatbelt as we reached Jermaine's driveway and rushed out the passenger side as soon as Dad stopped the car. I went around to the other side. "I'm good," he said, rising up out of the driver's seat. He took a few strides, to prove it, but he was swerving left just like the car. I didn't challenge him, but made sure I walked on his left side in case he fell. *He must be tired,* I figured.

The next day, Monday, class had just let out for lunch. My friend Davian was telling me about some prank he had pulled off when someone from the school told me to come to the office. I had no clue what was going on. About ten minutes later, Mom appeared. Her hair, which usually had every piece perfectly in place, was messy and she looked like she'd seen a ghost. "We have to go to the hospital. Now."

The mint-green walls at Martin Luther King Jr.–Harbor Hospital felt cold to the touch. The sound of the fluorescent lights humming gave me goosebumps. We walked down a hallway to a room at the end. There was a whiteboard on the wall to the right of the door with "Frank DeRozan" scribbled across it, along with a short list of other names I didn't recognize. Inside there were huge white curtains hanging from the ceiling like ghosts, separating the beds from one another. I took a deep breath, stepped into the room, and pulled back the curtain. There was my dad, lying still. His eyes lit up when he saw us but he couldn't really move. There were all these cables coming out of him and he was attached to a machine that beeped every few seconds. I wanted to pull the cables and grab my dad and run out of there. I'd never seen him like this. He looked beat. Defeated. Human, not the Big Dog I'd grown up with.

A doctor came into the room and explained that dad had suffered a stroke. He was going to recover, the doc said, but would need to rest. It wasn't until years later that I made the connection between his erratic behavior the day before, that his left side had been temporarily paralyzed as a result of the stroke. That tough, stubborn motherfucker. I'd watched him drive an hour from Compton to Hollywood, sit there and play a game of dominoes with one hand, and then drive us an hour back home. I didn't think nothing of it at the time because he was always putting on a brave face like that—even if it came to the point of pure denial. "Everything's fine, everything's fine." Everything was always fine. It made me realize how strong he was. That man was a bull.

The doctor left the room and Mom went to the vending machine down the hall. It was just us alone in the room. Dad motioned for me to come closer.

"Don't worry," he said. "I'm not gonna die until you make it."

CHAPTER 3

When I was five years old, my uncle Kevin was murdered. He was gunned down by a gang member from the Bloods. The bullet went straight through his heart. Uncle Kev was a postal worker, a hardworking blue-collar type of guy. He was also, I'd learn at his funeral, one of the most influential members of the Crips in the city. They shut down parts of the city for the ceremony and it felt almost like a big parade to me, seeing hundreds of people come out to pay their respects and show love to my family. It was the first time I can remember being told somebody close to me had been killed. It was also the first funeral I had ever been to. Mom was torn up. She couldn't keep track of how many she'd been to over the years—one summer alone she attended twenty funerals. Years later I would realize that funerals were a dangerous place to be. I've been to funerals where there've been drive-by shootings and people were killed, violence breaking out everywhere while you're supposed to be grieving. Eventually, the local funeral homes started holding drive-by casket viewings to avoid having big crowds gather like sitting ducks.

◦   ◦   ◦

For the first nineteen years of my life, all I knew was darkness and anger. In that environment, the only way you knew how to deal with aggression was with aggression.

It's why I got into a lot of fights growing up. A *lot*. I looked for any reason I could find. When I was with my cousins, we'd fight. When I was at school, I'd fight. When I wasn't happy, I'd fight. You know, fighting to fight. "Resolve" and "reasoning" weren't in my vocabulary back then. It got so bad that I was expelled from my grade school, Marian Anderson Elementary.

Whenever I got into a fight at school, they'd make me call my parents. I'd be marched into the principal's office, a cavernous room with gray concrete walls and industrial lighting. The school would make me call my parents—I always made sure to call Mom, the softer of the two. "Ma, let's not tell Dad," I would beg her once the dust settled. "All right, all right," she'd say. "Just don't do that shit again."

There was always another fight. Eventually Mom got fed up and told the school that the next time I got into a fight she wasn't going to answer. "Have him call his dad instead," she said. The next fight I got into—I can't remember what sparked it, they're all blurred together in my memories—my stomach sank when the school told me I had to call my dad and not my mom. He had to leave work to come and get me.

"The hell you fighting for!?" he went off on me during the car ride home, more disappointed than angry. You know how it's kind of scarier when a parent *isn't* yelling?

"I dunno. To fight."

"Can't you see you're missing school because of it?"

That didn't seem like such a bad thing to me. I couldn't stand school. I hated every class. I was too busy questioning everything to follow the lesson plans and wasn't one to sit back and listen to the teachers. We'd be reading a book about history and I'd be flipping through it, saying, "Teacher, how'd they know this happened?" No teacher had patience for me. They all used to say I asked too many questions. The best part about school was seeing your friends. Like with my cousins, I had a close circle of friends in the neighborhood. No one was closer than Davian. He and I were one and the same. We liked the same music, we liked the same girls, we both loved hoopin'. We'd meet up at the same spot in the morning on the way to school, hang out after school was finished, then talk on the phone at night, comparing which girls we wanted to ask out and ragging on each other. Typical kid stuff.

His family was heavily entrenched in the Crip community on our block. And his parents were young, at least ten years younger than mine. It wasn't until I was older that I realized how blessed I was to have had older parents who were more mature and helped keep me out of trouble. Davian, like many of my friends, didn't have that advantage.

Like my cousins, Davian was a jokester—I remember we used to make prank phone calls when we were young. Davian would look up a random number in the phone book and I would dial the numbers.

"Hey, is this Jimmy?" one of us would ask. The voice on the other end would say something like, "Um, yes . . . who the hell this is?" confused and skeptical after hearing a kid's voice on the line.

"The same Jimmy that owes me money?!" we'd yell, laughing like hyenas when they'd hang up. The angrier the person got, the harder we laughed.

Like my cousins, it was our shared experiences growing up in the neighborhood, navigating a world where just making it through to the next day is an achievement, that made us close.

Davian and I had another thing in common: We both liked to fight. And we were both good at it. Davian was much smaller than me, but he knew how to use his fists and had the heart of a lion. We did some damage back in our day. Our record in street fights was impressive.

But my dad wasn't having any of it. His stroke had mellowed him a bit, but he was still the Big Dog and I didn't want to get bit. By middle school, once basketball had morphed into an obsession, Dad would explain that to play for the school team I needed to *be in school*. "You ain't gonna be able to play if you keep fighting," he explained to me. That was all I needed to be told.

o o o

I've spent many hours trying to figure out how I was able to avoid going down the wrong path. It could have happened so easily. But I was one of the lucky ones. I had a protective circle around me, placed there by my mom and dad. Mom had always been overprotective—I was her only child, her miracle baby, and she wasn't going to let anything happen to me. She had already seen enough family members killed by gang violence and wasn't about to add her son to the list.

It wasn't really even an option for me. At my parents' request, my cousins were always trying to make sure I stayed out of trouble. All of them, down the line, let it be known that I wasn't to be involved in any of the gangster shit. "Nah, not D." They shielded me from it as best they could when I was a kid, and at the same time made sure I knew that I wasn't obligated to do what everybody else was doing. Because it's so easy to get caught up in it. I saw so many friends—dudes who *didn't* have both parents in their lives and people watching out for them—fall into trouble. So many. Whereas some people might feel pressure or obligation to join a gang, it was never pushed on me like that. My family was so respected and deeply entrenched in that world that I was afforded the freedom to stay out.

Besides, nobody wanted to have to answer to my mom or my aunties. They didn't play around. Like the majority of women in my life, they were aggressive figures. And you didn't want to disappoint them. I can't tell you how many times I would hear one of my cousins say, "Nah, D, I'm not about to deal with your mama."

I never felt the need to rebel. I'd seen the reality of that gang life. It was *too* real. I think most people don't see the reality in it until something bad happens, like my uncle Kevin's murder. Even at five I could see the impact it had on my mom and my family. It tore them up. My mom had lost countless loved ones, and I wanted to keep that from happening to her anymore. Between my cousins sheltering me and my love for my parents, I didn't need much more motivation to stay on a clean path.

º º º

"Hey, D, Grandma wants you!" my cousin DeShaun hollered at me. I was eight years old and it was a typical hazy Sunday afternoon in September. I was playing with my cousins at Grandma's house—earlier in the day we'd broken into the local school gym to shoot some hoops before settling down in front of the TV to watch football. DeShaun said Grandma was across the street, at a sports-bookie joint where she'd go to catch the races. Grandma, like my mom and auntie, loved to bet on horses. Small-time stuff.

I bolted out the door and ran to the bookie joint, which was in a house painted a dark shade of pink. Older people were always going in and out.

I knocked on the door and a man in a plaid jacket and a Kangol golf hat, like the kind Sam Jackson's character wore in *Jackie Brown*, let me in and pointed me toward Grandma. Inside there were a lot of TVs, and a round card table in the middle of the living room, with white sheets of paper stacked on top with the names and numbers of the horses and the race schedules printed out. I walked toward Grandma, past a small row of broken pinball and arcade games. Grandma, Mom, and Auntie Donna were cheery—I could tell they had just won. Usually when Grandma won, she'd give me a dollar. (I told you Grandma played favorites.)

"DeMar, c'mon, you take this," she said, placing a crisp dollar bill in my hand.

"Girls . . . ?" She raised an eyebrow.

My mom and auntie each handed me a dollar.

"All right, go on now," Grandma said. "The ice cream truck will be here in no time."

I thanked Grandma, told her I loved her, and headed toward the door. I wanted to show off my cash to DeShaun and the rest of them back at the house. *Maybe I'll get two sugar cones with strawberry ice cream.* I was budgeting in my head. *Nah—one cone, two scoops. Nah. Two cones AND two scoops.* Then—*KABLAM!!*—a huge blast came from the front of the house. The door crashed down and a small army of LAPD officers filled the doorframe. Some people scurried away like bugs. Others, like me, froze. To my eight-year-old eyes, the cops looked like they were a SWAT team. They were clad in black, visors covering their eyes, guns drawn, and yelling at us.

"Everybody on the ground NOW!!"

I didn't know what the fuck was going on. Before I could ask my mom, the cops had us all lying face-down on the floor—me, Mama, Auntie Donna, and Grandma. Instead of ice cream, I got caught in a full-on police raid. By the letter of the law this place was operating illegally. But I was eight—I had no idea what that meant. To me, this was just the house where everybody hung out and watched sports.

Grandma was on the ground next to me. I must have looked scared as hell. "It's all right, baby," she said. "Everything is going to be fine." Turns out this wasn't the first time the house had been raided. And it was far from the last.

If it wasn't the gangs, it was the police.

When I was in high school, a friend of mine was shot and killed by police while he was sleeping in his car. I don't know what happened, but the story that went around was that it was early in the morning and the cops were trying to wake him up. He was out cold, and the windows had fogged up a bit. They knocked on the window and yelled at him to get up and out of the vehicle. When he didn't respond, they shot him right through the glass. He died instantly. In their report, the cops had said that, because of the fogged-up window, they couldn't tell if he was pointing a gun at them or not. At least that's what I heard.

It was impossible to avoid run-ins with the police in those days. As a teenager I was in countless situations where one of my friends would roll by the house and pick me up to hang out. We'd get pulled over by the police—a group of Black kids in a car seemed to be all the reason they needed—and the officer would look into the driver's window.

"Any weapons in the car?"

I'd be sitting in the back seat, and look down and see a pistol peeking out from underneath the driver's seat. Or a TEC-9 in someone's gym bag. I'd think, *Man, if they check, it's game over.* I can't tell you how many times something like that would happen.

The dynamics with police were always conflicting for me, because Dad worked for the city and knew most of the police officers who patrolled Compton. I'd be walking past some bullshit traffic stop, and the cop would give me a stare and say, "Hey, aren't you Frank's son?" Dad would talk to me about the police from a different perspective than I was used to hearing. (Remember: Compton is where N.W.A's famous track "Fuck tha Police" was born.) Don't get me wrong, Dad would warn me to keep my cool when I was around cops. He knew the risks of being Black in America when it comes to policing. He told me to be careful out there, but he'd also explain how necessary police are in society and whatnot. I listened, but it was hard to see the good in the police. I saw how they treated people, dragging innocent kids out of cars for no reason, accusing regular working folks of having a little bit of weed on them or something, and tearing their car apart—or worse—while searching for it. You become conditioned to avoid them. You see police, you think, *Damn, I hope they don't bother me* and want to turn the other way. But if you do, it just makes them more suspicious and gives them reason to harass you. It was like damned if you do, damned if you don't. The cops ride by you, you make eye contact with them, and then—*CLICK*—just like that, they flick the sirens on and you see those flashing lights.

Sometimes you don't even have to look. They're already waiting for you.

In 2010, before my second season in the NBA, my cousins MC, James, DeShaun, and I were having a late-night meal in L.A. at Roscoe's Chicken and Waffles, a popular restaurant chain, following a gym session. We left the restaurant at about 11, filed into a black Cadillac Escalade parked outside, and headed off to drop me off at my parents' house about a half-hour away. We'd made it one block when we saw the red and blue lights flashing and heard the siren calling for us to pull over. I swear, it was like they had been waiting for us. Like they'd seen a group of young Black men together and saw an opportunity to pounce. We pulled over, and two white officers approached the car. "Okay, what do you have in here? Any guns? Drugs?" They shined their Maglite into my eyes and throughout the interior of the car. They started going through our backpacks and told us to empty our pockets. I was fuming and felt humiliated. They didn't find a thing—because there was nothing to be found. "Let's see your arms, then," one of the officers said after the search came up empty. "Show me your tattoos." They inspected our tattoos, looking for gang markings, asking what this one means and what that one means. "That says 'Blessed One,'" I said, pointing to a tattoo on my wrist. "And that one says 'Loyalty.'" The officers huddled outside the car.

"Well, look," one of them said, "*somebody* is going to jail tonight."

It was like they were bored and needed something to do. Or that they had orders from their boss to meet some quota of arresting innocent Black men that night. Whatever it was, they weren't joking. So DeShaun went to jail that night. He volunteered, and wound up spending six or seven hours there before he was released.

In 2020, when I heard that Compton was holding its own rally to protest police brutality in America and the death of George Floyd—the innocent Minnesota man who'd been killed when an officer held a knee to his throat for more than nine minutes during a shady traffic stop—I knew I had to be there. They called it the Compton Peace Walk, and I was proud to march with my people, including my friends Russell Westbrook and Kendrick Lamar, who's also from Compton. Even today, whenever I go back there I worry I'll get bothered by the police. You just never know. As soon as I hit the freeway to begin the hour-or-so drive home, I let out a huge sigh of relief. Every time.

○   ○   ○

I never knew how to process any of this. The killings, the gang violence, the police brutality and blatant injustice. We never had grief counselors. Never talked about what trauma is and how to cope. You just swept your feelings aside, or, worse, bottled them up and put a cap on it. That way, you hope it doesn't spray everywhere when the bottle is shaken.

The grief led to pain, which bred confusion. The more confused I got the angrier I became, until I found myself damn near always on the verge of rage.

My only therapy at the time—and I would never have called it that—was to channel all of it into basketball. Sports became something I could lean on, an outlet for my pain. I could take my frustrations out on the court, or on the rim, but I knew that wasn't an option for everybody. As I got older, I would be hanging with my friends, who would be so deep in all this violence and other bad shit for the simple reason that they didn't have nothing else. Meanwhile, I already felt fucked up if I let my dad down by not figuring out a fucking basketball move. How would I feel if I let him down by getting into some real trouble?

I started noticing a difference in myself. As I took basketball more and more seriously and realized that I had a shot at a life that was better than the one I'd been living, I became more detached from the people outside my immediate circle. I didn't want to become close with people, because I didn't know when they were going to disappear. And I didn't want to feel that pain. *I don't know if you'll be gone tomorrow. If you die, it's only going to hurt more if I open myself up to you now.* I was guarded.

I always used to think about that set-up in the movie *Back to the Future*, where the main character keeps the picture of his family in his back pocket. And over time the people in the picture begin to fade away. That's what my life began to feel like. I thought about it so much that, as a kid, I hated taking pictures with people from the block.

I never wanted to be sitting at home, years later, and be looking at all of these photos of friends I'd seen die too young. I didn't want to reminisce, and to be able to pinpoint the exact day and moment I remembered losing somebody, and to know that they're not here anymore. Sometimes, when I look at old photos today, all I see are faded faces.

CHAPTER 4

Despite all the dangers of my environment, I was scared to leave home.

By the time I was in the eighth grade, I had multiple high schools recruiting me to play basketball. My reputation was growing after I won a national summer league title with an AAU team called the SoCal All-Stars that featured another future NBA pro, Brandon Jennings, at point guard. Suddenly, I had options. I was considering Rancho Dominguez High School, where two guys who'd played in the NBA, Tayshaun Prince and Tyson Chandler, had attended, as well as Sierra High School, a private Catholic school with pristine facilities and only a hundred students. When I went to visit those schools, I knew they weren't for me. It was just too different than anything I knew. I also thought about going to a school outside Los Angeles—outside California, even—like Oak Hill Academy, a Virginia private school known for producing NBA players like Carmelo Anthony, Kevin Durant, and Rajon Rondo. (My friend Brandon Jennings, who was also from Compton and would end up getting chosen one pick after me in the NBA draft, also went to Oak Hill.) But deep down, I knew it was never an option for me to leave home. I wasn't ready. Besides, I had grown up in a place where loyalty is valued above everything else.

So I stayed nearby and chose Compton High School, which was almost literally across the street from my house. Unlike those other schools, Compton High didn't exactly have a long history of producing NBA talent. In 2001 a player from Compton High, Jeff Trepagnier, was drafted, and he lasted a few seasons. Before that you have to go back to the seventies to find another dude from the school who stepped on an NBA floor. It also didn't have a history of winning basketball games. But I trusted my abilities, and I wanted to play for the school's coach, Tony Thomas, a no-nonsense guy who demanded accountability. My dad always had a good radar about people. Who was genuine, who was a snake. He liked Tony, a math teacher at the school, and trusted him to carry the baton—Dad let it be known that the farther I went in my hoops journey the more he'd have to pass along coaching responsibilities as my game advanced. With Tony, Dad knew I'd be in capable hands. Tony's father had been the school's first Black head coach. Tony loved the game and knew it well.

Tony was promised the head coaching job at Compton High just in time for my freshman year in 2005. We talked about putting Compton basketball on the map—playing in the major state tournaments, recruiting other talented players, and rewriting the school's reputation. Turns out there was a lot of backroom politics going on with the school's administration. My freshman year came and went and Tony was nowhere to be seen. Sophomore year, same deal. In the meantime, our team was pretty terrible. I was playing for another coach and he was all over the place and kept changing our playing style from game to game. I thought about leaving. Sure, I loved going to school in the neighborhood I grew up in, and all of my friends, like Davian, were at Compton High. But by that point I was so laser-focused on getting to the NBA and the clock was ticking. I wanted the exposure that friends at other L.A. area high schools were getting. With exposure came college scholarships. But no major scouts were coming to Compton High games.

Finally, in the summer after my sophomore year, the school hired Tony. Immediately things took off. He implemented a fast-paced style and soon we were running teams out of the gym. We started playing in bigger tournaments and winning games. My junior year we won the Moore League title for the first time in school history. There was a ton of buzz in the community. Our games became events, which had been unheard of—it had always been Compton High's football team that drew big crowds. One of the school's most famous alumni, the rapper The Game, would come by—you couldn't miss him, he bought matching Dodge Challengers for him and his entire crew—and show up at the football games, which were always popular in our city. But that was changing. Suddenly the gym was packed for every basketball game. People were coming up to me everywhere I went, congratulating me on the team's success and on my play. I won't lie, it felt amazing to be doing so well. I was *dominating* the high school circuit. I felt unstoppable. But I was never one to seek attention; it made me uncomfortable. My dad started walking around Compton wearing a shirt that read "DeMar's Dad" across the back. I was so embarrassed. But what can I say, he was proud that I was making a name for myself.

○   ○   ○

Each day my NBA dream felt closer to reality. And each day I wanted it worse than the day before.

We had a family friend, Leroy "Chico" Brown, a notorious ex-gangster from Compton. Chico was an influential member of the Corner Poccet Crips. He grew up on Nord Street and was always tight with my uncles, and he acted like a big brother to my auntie Donna. I always knew him as "Uncle Chico."

After my uncle Kevin was killed, Chico took it upon himself to help look out for the family. As I grew older we spent more time together. He'd drive me to and from basketball games and make sure I veered away from trouble. Chico was a bright dude who knew how to make a buck—legitimately or otherwise. He once told me that if some of the gang leaders from his day had worked in the corporate world instead of the world of organized crime, they'd have risen through the ranks to CEO.

Chico was stout and sturdy, with a round head he shaved bald as a pool ball; he looked the part of an ex–football player. When I was a kid, he was a familiar face in the neighborhood. He was always lending a hand with whatever he could—coaching local sports teams, making sure kids got to school, offering rides, settling beefs—you name it. The whole time, he was making amends with his own past.

In the eighties and nineties, Compton was in the throes of a crack epidemic. The drug was destroying the city. Once people were hooked, they'd do anything to get more. Kids were left alone while their parents tried to score. Sometimes the parents never returned home, sent to jail or killed along the way while the children grew up without a mom or dad around. We used to hear stories—cautionary tales—about how someone's grandma sold her house to get money to buy crack. Shit like that. It tore families apart. It tore Compton apart. And Uncle Chico felt at least partially responsible.

For the bulk of my childhood Uncle Chico was in prison, serving time for one of California's most famous drug busts.

I was in the seventh grade when Uncle Chico returned home from jail. At the time, I had no idea about any of his past. It wasn't until I was an adult that I learned about his history with the gangs. It was hard to believe: From everything I could see, Chico was building up the community, not tearing it down. He emerged from his time locked up determined to make a positive impact on Compton, to turn his own life around by focusing on improving the lives of those around him. He started a business called Ex-Contracting, a construction company that gave jobs to ex-convicts who couldn't find work. He also opened a pair of youth centers in the city and ran an after-school program with access to sports, music studios, and workshops. It gave kids a place to go after school instead of hanging out in the streets and getting caught up in the middle of God-knows-what.

While re-establishing himself in the community as an activist and gang-interventionist, Uncle Chico developed a relationship with some people connected with the Los Angeles Clippers organization. He'd manage to arrange for kids like me to go to Clippers games and sometimes even meet the players. We'd be sitting up in the nosebleed seats, but it didn't matter. It was a mind-blowing experience to be that close to NBA hoops. Maybe it's because Chico saw what my dad saw—that I had a real shot of making it through basketball—or maybe because he'd always said he would look after my family after Uncle Kev's death, but while I was in middle school he took me all around Los Angeles. He exposed me to a whole other world. We'd visit people like Mark Wahlberg, whose youth foundation did work with Chico, and Penny Marshall, the famous director, who used to be a fixture at Clippers games. I think she had known of Uncle Chico from back in the day, when he used to sit courtside at Laker games. As he was writing this new chapter in his life, Penny helped him take a step into the entertainment business by getting his production company, Snowfall Films, off the ground. We used to go to Penny Marshall's house sometimes. At the time I didn't question any of it. I was just a kid riding around with my uncle while he visited his friend Penny. But looking back, it's so crazy. What was I, a nobody kid from Compton, doing in the Hollywood Hills mansion of the woman who directed *Big*? I would try to keep it cool, but it was tough. Her house was next-level. It felt like the size of my entire school, and everything looked like it was from the pages of a home decor magazine. Her kitchen was made to look like a retro fifties diner, and she had a massive pool in her backyard that overlooked Los Angeles.

But what I really remember is her basement. When I would show up with Uncle Chico, Penny used to grab my hand and excitedly rush us downstairs.

"Come this way," she'd direct us. "You *have* to see what I just got!"

Once down the steps it was like walking into the world's most impressive—and crowded—sports memorabilia shop. Every inch of the walls was covered with framed photos of Penny posing with legends like Muhammad Ali. She would walk me around the room proudly. There were game-worn jerseys, sneakers, hats, bobblehead dolls, and game-used sporting equipment lining every square inch of the enormous room—all of it autographed. There were display cases from floor to ceiling filled with baseballs and basketballs signed by every notable player you could think of. It was just the wildest shit I'd ever seen. There was one item in particular I'll never forget: a section of the original Los Angeles Forum court, signed by Kareem, Magic, and other famous Lakers who had graced the iconic hardwood that I used to watch obsessively on those grainy VHS tapes. After Penny's death in 2018, her collection of hoops relics was donated to the Naismith Basketball Hall of Fame. It was the largest single donation of memorabilia in the sixty-five-year history of the Hall.

It wasn't just movie stars that Uncle Chico took me to meet. He knew NBA players, too. One player he was close to was Sam Cassell, who played point guard for the Clippers at the time. Cassell was like a cartoon character come to life. He talked a mile a minute and was always emphasizing whatever he was saying with dramatic hand gestures. Uncle Chico told Cassell that I was on my way up in the L.A. hoops scene and Cassell seemed more than happy to talk my ear off about the game of basketball.

"Kid, what do you know about the pump-fake?" he asked one day in his hurried voice, obviously eager to tell me all about it regardless of my answer.

"Don't worry, don't worry, I'm gonna tell you what to do," he said, jumping up out of his chair, a scowl across his face as he transported his mind to the basketball court.

"Man, you get to your spot, kid, you hit a motherfucker wit' this."

Holding an imaginary ball at hip level, he raises it above his head like he's about to take a jump shot and lowers it back down again in a flash.

"You hit him wit' it again . . ." I swear he was starting to sweat.

"They gonna jump. I *know* they gonna jump. Every time. Then once you got them in the air, you wait until they land and just shoot it over their head."

He takes an imaginary shot and I watch its arc through the living room. Swish.

"Every time, I'm telling you."

He would give me secrets to the mid-range game, which later became my calling card in the NBA.

"Man, you don't need but two dribbles any direction," he cackled, "then you feel the bump—notice I didn't say 'push,' I said 'bump.' That's all the space you need. Bucket."

I took it all in. Whether it was Penny Marshall or Sam Cassell, I used to be so intrigued when I was around successful people that I rarely even said a word. I just paid attention. People used to think I was shy. Nah. I was too busy listening.

On the ride down the 101 on the way back to Compton I'd stare at the dunes out the window and replay the conversations over and over again in my head. *Hit a motherfucker wit' this. Then hit 'em again.* These lessons were giving me a whole new perspective. I don't think Sam realizes how much he was teaching me during those conversations. I was being given access to the hoops brain of a real NBA player. With each move I watched on the court I was gaining an understanding of the reason and intention behind it. It was like unlocking a new level.

○   ○   ○

The summer circuit was always a big deal in Southern California. Every weekend was another event, whether it's a camp, AAU tournament, or heated pickup games. The summertime is when I went to battle with and against all the top L.A. high school players from that time: James Harden, Jrue Holiday, Paul George, and Klay Thompson, to name a few. Guys I'm still close with today. We spent so much time together back then that it becomes like a brotherhood among top prospects whose paths had crossed since we were little kids. My dad was close with Klay's dad, Mychael, a first overall draft pick who played in the NBA until he was thirty-seven.

My middle school AAU team, the SoCal All-Stars, disbanded by the time I was in high school. One of my teammates and my closest friend from that team was Romeo Miller, a talented guard and the son of famous rapper Percy Miller, aka Master P. AAU was an important launching pad to the NBA. It was just as important as what school you went to, when it came to exposure and a chance to play against the country's best players. So when we were in high school we were looking for a new team to join when P came up with the idea to start his own team, the P. Miller All-Stars. Rome and I joined the team and we were good right from the jump. It was wild how generous P was with us. He would fly us on a private plane to play out-of-state games. When we'd land, these big luxury buses would be waiting to take us to a five-star hotel. It was like a taste of the NBA life. I couldn't believe it.

It was so disconnected from life as I had known it that it just didn't feel real. He gave everyone on the team cell phones—it was my first phone, a T-Mobile Sidekick with the keyboard pad on it. I'm telling you, we were livin' large.

The more we played together, the closer my friendship with Romeo got. Rome was a big star in his own right. Using the name "Lil' Romeo," he hit number three on the Billboard charts by the time he was just twelve years old. By my freshman year of high school he already had three albums out, all hitting the top 100. I'll never forget bringing Rome by my high school one day. It was mass chaos. The kids just swarmed him and followed him anywhere he went, like he was the Pied Piper. I used to love it because he got so much attention that it was one of the few opportunities where I could just slip into the background.

I always looked forward to hanging out at Romeo's house. He lived in a big-ass L.A. mansion with his dad. And he had everything a kid could ever want. Arcade games, an indoor basketball court with a weight room attached, a sick pool, a music recording studio, and the biggest TV I'd ever seen. His dad used to throw parties for the team. At one of them I positioned myself at the door and told everyone who showed up that there was a five-dollar entrance fee. I went home with a pocket full of cash that night.

I felt an amazing sense of freedom at Romeo's place. It meant that I could get out of Compton for the day, and not have to hang around the streets and try to stay out of trouble. I really appreciated what his friendship meant to me. Visiting Romeo's crib gave me even more motivation to keep pursuing my dreams—I felt so close to success and didn't want to let it out of my sight. But it also taught me not to value materialistic things. As much as Romeo had, I saw how he still couldn't escape life's problems. His dad had every car you could imagine and was rich beyond belief. But he still went through ups and downs as much as the next man. Being so young, and having nothing, it was easy for me to think, *Oh, shit, I'll do* anything *for this.* But when you're around that type of material wealth, you learn pretty quickly that it ain't it. There's more to life. People can hide behind money and fame, but at the end of the day you still have to face yourself in the mirror. And if you're not happy with the person staring back at you then what does all the wealth in the world matter? That always stuck with me, and when I first made it to the league I never forgot it. I didn't rush to buy a big mansion or a fleet of cars, or some of the other things people spend their first millions on. I wasn't trippin'. Hell, for the first three years I was in the NBA I still liked sleeping on my mom's couch when I'd come home to visit.

I was loyal to the P. Miller All-Stars. Romeo, P, and the whole team had shown me so much love and granted me access into a whole different world. But the bigger I got, the more I was getting tugged and pulled in every direction—even by my own family. For the longest time, my brother, Jermaine, wanted me to suit up for a local AAU team he was coaching. I got the feeling someone probably promised him something if he could recruit me. I remember being in the car with him and my dad one afternoon leaving a tournament at Lakewood High School in Long Beach. Jermaine was upset that I wasn't willing to leave Romeo's team. "You need to come play for *us*," he said.

"Man, I'm not doing *nothin'* I don't wanna do."

That set him off. "See, that's what's wrong with you," he began, one hand on the steering wheel, the other pointing back at me in the back seat. "You just don't listen." He kept going on and on. Dad just sat in the front passenger seat, taking it all in. I was getting so mad. "Man, pull over, I'll fucking walk home," I said.

Jermaine started driving crazy, swerving all over the place as he tried to reach back to hit me. Then he slammed on the brakes.

"Fine, get the fuck out."

We were across the street from the Compton Swap Meet, about an hour's walk from home. I got up out of the car on the passenger's side and reached into the back seat to pull out my backpack. Next thing I know, Jermaine had come around from the driver's side and took a big swing at me. It was on. We started fighting in the middle of the street, spilling over onto the curb then back in front of the car. Other cars were honking at us to get out of the way, and Dad got out of the car to try to break us up, but he couldn't. Eventually, he gave up, got behind the wheel, and drove off. Jermaine and I just stood there watching Dad disappear into the distance. I ended up calling my mom to come pick us both up.

⋄ ⋄ ⋄

It was 8 o'clock on the morning of May 3 during my junior year. I was headed to first period when I felt the cell phone vibrating in the pocket of my sweatpants. It was my mom calling. I picked up the phone.

"Ma, I told you, I'll be home after sch—"

"It's Grandma," she cut me off. "She's gone."

Grandma had some form of cancer, I can't remember which, and the writing had been on the wall for some time. Still, it didn't make the news any easier to digest. I loved my grandma, and I don't think there was anybody I felt safer with in the world. I didn't know how to process the news, so I reacted as I normally did: I got angry and withdrew. I didn't want to talk to nobody.

Mom said one of my cousins was going to come pick me up from school and take me to meet her and Dad at the hospital. So I made my way to Tony's classroom, where he taught math. The door was locked, and I fell back against the wall and slid to the floor where I sat and waited. A few moments later I heard sneakers slapping across the vinyl floors and looked up to see Tony running down the hallway. "Hey, Coach," I managed to say.

"Man, sorry, Deebo, but I gotta go," he said as he rushed away. Turns out his mother had died that same morning. And what's crazy is that, six days after Grandma died, my grandfather passed away, too.

○   ○   ○

It was hard to separate my growing love for basketball from my thoughts of Grandma. After she passed, whenever I watched a game on TV I would think of her. It seemed like my happiest memories as a kid took place at Grandma's house. One of my favorite things to do was watch the Laker games live on Channel 9 with her, my dad, and my cousins. Back when I was a kid the team had just moved past the Magic Johnson era, with players like Nick Van Exel and Vlade Divac showing up on the television at Grandma's.

But my favorite player growing up was Kobe Bryant. No figure loomed larger in L.A. basketball in those days than Kobe. He was my imagination—the guy I used to pretend to be more than anybody else when I was on the court.

In 1996, just before my seventh birthday, the Lakers traded Divac for the thirteenth pick in the draft—Kobe. I remember the whole neighborhood was buzzing about the fact that he was selected straight out of high school and just seventeen years old. In the papers and on TV they were saying that he had the makings to be the NBA's next big star. He came into the league with a shaved head and all the swagger in the world. I couldn't wait to see what he could do. He didn't play much at first, which made me want to root for him even more.

There was one moment during Kobe's rookie season that I'll never forget watching live. All these years later, it's still my favorite basketball memory of him. It's May 6, 1997, and the Lakers are trailing the Utah Jazz, with Karl Malone and John Stockton, 3–1 in the second round of the playoffs. In Game 5, with the season on the line and the score tied at 89, eighteen-year-old Kobe brings the ball up the court with a chance to win the game. I got up and stood in front of the TV. With four seconds on the clock, he sprints to the right elbow and pulls up for a jumper. Airball. Malone catches the ball as time expires. I wanted Kobe to hit that shot *so bad*. In overtime, down by two with forty-two seconds to go, Kobe rises up for a three at the top of the key. Airball. The Lakers still trail by three with eleven seconds to go. Nick Van Exel, the Lakers point guard, takes a screen, draws a double-team, and passes out to Kobe. He starts shooting before the ball lands in his hands. The shot goes up. Airball. I damn near cried watching him walk off the court after the buzzer sounded.

The rest of the night the same thought replayed in my head: *He wanted it. He kept wanting to take the shot.* I was so impressed by that. Kobe never backed down from the moment. The next day,

I was out at a store and there was a TV on in the background playing the local news. They were talking about Kobe. The media had all of this negative stuff to say—how this kid should have never had the ball in those moments, how he left school too early and wasn't ready. *It must be so strange to hear that kind of shit said about you publicly like that,* I thought.

But Kobe didn't let any of that break him. First game of the next season, the Lakers played Utah. I remember because it was Halloween night. Kobe scored 23 points and the Lakers won by 17. It was amazing to watch how he bounced back in his second year, becoming the youngest player to make an All-Star team, and just kept getting better from there.

I idolized Kobe and began to model my game after him. In high school, when Kobe was letting his 'fro grow out a bit, I started letting mine grow out, too. I would push my hair back to make it look like his.

So you can imagine how dope it was when, in 2006 when I was fifteen years old, I was invited to attend one of his basketball camps. Each summer he held a weeklong training program in L.A. for top prospects. It was a chance to not only meet Kobe but talk to him and work on the court with him. There's a picture of Kobe sitting in a folding chair, talking to a group of campers about four rows deep. You can see teenage Klay Thompson, Jrue Holiday, Tyreke Evans, Brandon Jennings, and other future NBA dudes in the picture. Front row and center is me, staring at Kobe. Locked in. Once, when I was working on a footwork drill, he came up to me. We started talking about certain moves. I asked what he did to work on his jab-step, the intentions behind the move. He was definitely intimidating, but the more we talked about hoops, and the more I picked his brain on the intricacies of his game, the more comfortable I felt.

My junior year in high school, he sent me a text message after a particularly big game: "Way to go, keep that shit up." I lost my mind, showing it off to Davian and all my friends, who didn't believe it was real. After another big game, he called me and told me I could reach out anytime I needed advice, or just to talk. That he was there for me. Soon as he hung up I called my mom. "Mama, do you know who just called!?!?"

We had a mutual acquaintance, this friend named Dre, who used to let me know if Kobe was in town and in the gym somewhere. I would show up to watch him work out, and most of the time Kobe would wave for me to join him.

I don't know what made him want to allow me into his world and get close. Maybe it was because I was always asking the right questions, and I was a careful listener. With Kobe, you had to be. Everything he said was so cryptic and mysterious. You had to really unpack what he was saying in order to understand it.

Kobe was constantly giving out clues, like basketball was a fucking who-done-it mystery. Like we were all characters in *Murder on the Orient Express*. But you listen and you act like, "Oh, cool, cool." And then go off and try to put the clues together.

That was Kobe.

Our relationship got tighter and tighter throughout high school. By the end of my senior year at Compton High, I was the third-ranked high school player in the country behind only Jrue Holiday and B.J. Mullins. That summer, 2008, Kobe was training like crazy in preparation for the Beijing Olympics and invited me to train with him and join him in pickup runs at Palisades High School. Kobe helped me understand what was next. How once I reached the next level I wouldn't be able to coast on simply being a better athlete. How everybody would be coming after me because my name meant something. Even as our connection grew throughout my career, I can tell you that it never really felt "normal" to me. How could it? He was my whole imagination as a child. Kobe gave me the foundation of what type of hooper I wanted to be. If it wasn't for him, I wouldn't be where I'm at today.

When he found out we wore the same shoe size, he started sending me his signature Nike Kobe sneakers. I'm a big sneakerhead—I have a whole closet full, every shoe you can imagine in any color you like. My first sneakers were a pair of fake Air Jordan Concords that I bought at the Compton Swap Meet. I didn't care that they were fake, I was so proud to have them I wore them until there were holes in the bottom. When I went to college at USC, Kobe supplied every player on the team with Kobe sneakers in the red-and-yellow team colors. To this day, Kobe's are all I wear when I play. There was only one game when I didn't. It was in my third NBA season, a home game against the Lakers in February. A couple weeks earlier we were playing Vince Carter and the Nets. At some point in the game VC pointed at my shoes and said, "You ain't going to wear those when you play Kobe, are you?" I hadn't thought about that, but he made it sound like there was an unwritten rule that you don't wear your opponent's sneakers. It made sense. You think I'm about to give him a mental edge over *me*? Hell nah. So when it came time to suit up against him, I wore a pair of Jordan 10's instead. We walk onto the court before tip-off and the first thing Kobe says to me is: "The fuck you got on your feet?" He was pissed. That game he locked me *up*. I think I was 2-of-13 from the floor. The game came down to the wire, and with seven seconds on the clock the Lakers were inbounding down by one. Before the play, he walked past our bench and grinned. "You know you left me too much time, right?" The whistle blows and Kobe curls off a screen, catches the inbound pass, and takes a dribble into the corner directly in front of our bench. I chase after to double-team him but it's useless. He rises up into the air for a picture-perfect turnaround jumper. Game.

That was Kobe, too.

CHAPTER 5

One night, I'm riding shotgun in the car. It's 2008, about two months until the end of my senior year at Compton High. I had just been named to the McDonald's All American team and felt on top of the world, like my whole future was coming into focus. It was right there in front of me, so close that I could grab it. College, the NBA, following through on my promise to Grandma to take care of her family after she was gone.

We're just a few blocks from home and stopped at a red light when a silver truck with tinted windows appears from behind and pulls into the left-turn lane next to us. I look over. All of the windows are rolled down. Six dudes are crammed into the truck and all of them are staring right at us. They hold the stare as the light turns green and their vehicle starts its left turn. We head straight through the intersection, my cousin's foot heavy on the gas pedal. He looks into the rearview mirror to see that the truck is gone. "... the fuck? ..." I turn around and see it completing a U-turn and heading back behind us. My cousin doesn't say anything. He taps his driver's-side door and the panel pops off. Inside the door I can see several handguns. He grabs one, places it on the center console, and hovers his right hand above it. It's like he's saying, "I got this. *You* stay out of it as best you can."

I look into my side mirror. "Man, they coming," I say.

The truck catches up to us and pulls into the right lane on my side of the car. I held my breath—*Is this it?* I asked myself—and the truck takes a right turn down the next street.

We never saw it again.

"What the hell was that about!?" I asked.

"I have no idea," my cousin replied. He paused. "I think they were lost?" I wanted to laugh, even just to break the tension. I was so close to achieving my dreams. The stakes of simply making it through each day alive never seemed higher. In an environment surrounded by people hustling drugs and running around strapped with weapons, you can only avoid so much trouble. Fortunately, there had been so many times throughout high school where I was able to dodge it. Looking back, that incident with the truck was the last real situation I found myself in as a teenager where it seemed like everything I'd worked for could have been thrown away in an instant. We didn't know what was going to happen. Were they going to shoot at us? Did they even have guns? In the end nothing happened. But the paranoia, the uncertainty, the life-or-death of it all . . . we went through every day of our lives like that.

○   ○   ○

In the mid-2000s—and specifically during my last two years of high school, 2006–2008, Compton had become an even more dangerous place to live. In those years, there was a war going on within the city. No, really, you can look it up. It was gang warfare on a level even Compton hadn't seen before. The gangs were expanding rapidly, and there were a record number of shootings. All day and all night, the sights and sounds that would keep me awake at night as a kid were all amplified—gunshots, sirens, the constant hum of police helicopters. There were so many helicopters it was like the cops felt safer policing from the air. I could see why.

There were plenty of times during that period where I'd leave my school—which was in an established Crip area—at the end of the day and there'd be, no exaggeration, thirty dudes surrounding the school, waiting for certain people to leave. I had friends in gangs who would always be leaving school an hour early to avoid getting jumped when the bell rang. One night I got word that a friend of mine who sat next to me at school had been shot and killed. I remember going to class the next day and looking over to see his textbook, pencil, and papers and shit still on his desk like everything was normal. I suppose in a way it was.

The cycle was endless. I'd go to funerals for friends who had gone too deep into the gangs—or had been caught in the crossfire and died for the crime of being in the wrong place at the wrong time. I'd pay my respects, listening to the preacher talk about how we lost this life too young or that life too early, and bottle up the pain and frustration inside. I carried that anger with me everywhere I went.

I didn't think the game could have meant any more to me, but I built an even bigger appreciation for what the sport provided during those days when the city was at war with itself. I recognized that basketball could bring people together. And I loved the role that I could play in that. Blood, Crip, it didn't matter, people from all over Compton would come to watch my high school games. I realized that it wasn't every day that a player with my ability came out of Compton, that the list of dudes who had been ranked near the top nationwide was a short one. I represented my city with pride, and I felt that support right back. (It didn't hurt that my style was exciting to watch. Yeah, I was learning from guys like Kobe and Sam Cassell, working on my footwork and the finer points of the game. But I was a high-flyer back then. I liked to get up in the air, pull off acrobatic dunks, fly all over the court.)

At home games at Compton High they would have rival gangs use separate entrances. Before tip-off I would look up into the bleachers and try to count the number of different hoods represented, knowing they didn't get along with one another, to say the least. It felt like a superpower, to be able to bring these warring groups together to watch some hoop. And it's like they say: With great power comes great responsibility. I really felt that, and it helped keep me on my path.

° ° °

I carried so much baggage over the way I grew up and the friends and family I'd lost. But I knew that I didn't want to carry that baggage over to college and, more important, to the NBA.

So, near the end of my senior year, I tried to get away from all that negativity more and more. I spent more time with friends with big ambitions like myself. Like Rome. Or my friend Bernard, who I'm still tight with today. Bernard was on the Compton High basketball team with me, but his best sport was football, where he played both quarterback and cornerback. He was always working to make it out of Compton and had aspirations to be a professional football player. I watched him work relentlessly, get himself into college and try to make things happen at the next level. Injuries stopped his progress, and a torn ACL eliminated any chance of him getting drafted to the NFL. A few years later, when I was in Toronto playing for the Raptors, I arranged for him to get a tryout with the Toronto Argonauts of the Canadian Football League. In the tryout, he tore his knee again. Bernard was forced to put his athletic career in the back seat for good and has since started coaching football at the collegiate level. Point is, he was always trying to do something to better his situation. There was a huge drive in him, and by the time I was getting ready to graduate from Compton High, that's all I wanted to see in somebody close to me.

I started paying attention to the differences in people—those who wanted more, and those who didn't have the willingness, care, or imagination to improve their lives. It almost made it easier to grasp why I was losing people around me. Usually, it was because they were still in the streets, still doing negative things and surrounding themselves in a world of negativity. As strange as it sounds, being able to recognize that simple fact helped ease the pain of losing them. *What do you expect?* I would think. *You're content to stay in this environment, carrying on a dangerous life, what did you think was going to happen?* I saw that there was just nothing good that came from that world.

It was the losses I couldn't explain that really hurt.

※ ※ ※

When it came time to choose what college I would attend, I was fortunate to have plenty of options and received scholarship offers from most of the biggest programs in the country. I can't say I was the most engaged student academically, but I was able to get by and put myself in a position to be eligible for most scholarships. That was my whole life at that point: to get into a college and keep this NBA dream alive. Everything was about hoops. Anything else was secondary. I didn't even drink, and still don't to this day. People have their vices and that's cool, but growing up I saw too many people throw their lives away on booze or crack that it turned me off the shit completely. People on the block would turn to the bottle or to drugs as a way to hide from their reality. I had my own vice to hide behind: hoops.

As the college offers poured in, my parents made it clear that they would support whatever decision I made. By then my dad was more hands-off—he was always there for advice and was my number-one fan, but he told me it was my life and I should always be in the driver's seat.

I visited a few schools during my last year of high school. I remember getting flown out to the University of North Carolina to see the campus, athletic facilities and to meet Dean Smith, the legendary coach who had shepherded the likes of Michael Jordan, James Worthy, Vince Carter, and Jerry Stackhouse from college through to NBA stardom. The campus felt like walking onto the set of a movie. It felt high-class. A bit stuffy, even. Still, I could envision myself in that iconic Tar Heel blue, and I imagined continuing the legacy of two-guards who starred at UNC.

But like I've said, I'm as loyal as they come. My friend Rome had dreamed of playing college ball and worked his ass off to make it happen. But he was a bit undersized for Division One basketball and was having a hard time finding a school that would take him. Throughout my recruiting process, I had let it be known that whatever school I chose had to find a roster spot for Rome, too. Coach Smith refused. So I scratched them off my list.

I thought long and hard about what would be the most important thing I wanted out of my college basketball experience. At the time, I had the utmost confidence in what I could do on the court and knew that I was only going to get better with time. I felt there was a realistic chance that not only was I going to be drafted by an NBA team, but that I was likely good enough to declare for the draft after just one year of playing in the NCAA. Barring disaster, there was a countdown clock until my life in the NBA began, and it felt like that clock was ticking *fast*. My mother's lupus seemed to be getting worse each year, the pain growing more and more frequent, and I knew it would be hard for her to be traveling to watch me play once I made it to the league. Mom and Dad had always been my biggest cheerleaders. They never missed a game. So I decided that, above all else, I wanted to prioritize them. I wanted to give them the opportunity to watch me play as often as they could while I was in college.

The University of Southern California was one of the first schools to express interest in me. It was always an option in the back of my mind, if only because the campus was in Los Angeles, just a twenty-five-minute drive from my house. USC was more known for its football program, which just a few years earlier had appeared in three straight national-title games. Its basketball program had never gone further than the Elite Eight, which they had pulled off once in their one-hundred-year history. But I knew what I wanted, and that was a chance to play at home in front of my family one last time. To Mom and Dad, I was still their baby, but USC would offer me the best balance of independence, living on my own, while still just being a quick car ride from home. It felt good just to have the option. Besides, USC was willing to bring Rome on board and offer him a spot on the team. Done deal.

◦   ◦   ◦

I celebrated New Year's Eve beginning 2008 with Davian. We were always together, almost like a package deal. Outside of my parents, Davian was still the most important person in my life. We trusted each other completely. But as we had gotten older, he had started edging further into the gangbanging life. I had basketball to give me an outlet for my pain, but Davian didn't have that, or any other way out. I watched him over time subtly and gradually become more caught up in the lifestyle.

Three days after New Year's—January 3, 2008—Davian and I made a plan to hang at a mutual friend's house that night. Davian was going to roll by my place on Myrrh Street at about six o'clock, and then we were going to walk over together. I was lying on the couch in our living room, killing time while I waited for him. Six o'clock came and went, with no sign of Davian. He wasn't always the most punctual dude, so I kept waiting. I thought about calling him. Another hour passed. Eventually, I heard footsteps pounding on the pavement that got louder as they got closer to my front door. I got up to go open it, thinking, *Finally! Where the fuck you been!?* There was a hard, serious knock on the door. I opened it and one of my boys was slumped over, sweating, his chest puffing in and out as he tried to catch his breath. "Deebo," he managed to say, "They shot Davian. They shot him!"

Davian was already dead by the time I'd heard the news. He'd been shot during an argument while playing dice with some guys from another neighborhood. Killed at seventeen years old. His life taken over a fucking *dice game*. I couldn't process what I was hearing. For many years I blamed myself for his death. *Why didn't I just call him while I was waiting? Why didn't I just go pick him up?*

On the day of his funeral, I couldn't bring myself to go. Dad told me if I didn't I might wind up regretting it. But I just couldn't do it. I told him that it wasn't safe—which was true. There were brawls, shootings, killings on a daily basis at the time. With the gang presence everywhere, you knew there'd be gangs showing up to Davian's funeral and it wasn't far-fetched to expect the worst. I had been taking my college recruiting trips, deciding where to start my next chapter, and had worked *so fucking hard* to come this far. There was too much risk in going to the funeral, I said. But that wasn't it. The truth was, I couldn't stand the thought of seeing Davian in that casket. I just didn't want it to be real.

○　　○　　○

Why would they care about you? I had the phrase tattooed onto my right forearm. Every time I raise my shooting hand into form, I can read it.

I don't think most people understand how hard it is to make it out of the hood and how focused you have to be on that mission. It's just too easy to fall into the trappings of that environment. It may sound crazy, but that was the only way for people like us to make connections with others growing up. Everything was based on where you were from, and which crew you or your family rolled with. For a while, Davian found protection in that world.

By the time I was set to graduate from high school, I had seen many people I grew up around make similar choices. There was a revolving door, person after person, falling in with gangs, making bad decisions. It used to frustrate me so much to watch people throwing their lives away.

But now that I'm older, I've come to understand that, in a lot of ways, people back home were groomed to fail. It's like my dad always told me: "Nobody out there cares about you. Why would they?" And he was right. I was very grateful to be insulated in a supportive family. I knew that was a luxury that many people around me didn't have.

I remember so many instances of going to a friend's house—from when I was a little kid all the way through high school—and their mom would be sitting on a couch strung out on drugs, staring into the distance, or would hit up her kid for drug money. Their parents would treat them like shit, like they didn't matter. I had a friend in the neighborhood whose dad used to talk crazy to him. "You ain't *shit*," his dad would be yelling at him, drunk or high. "I don't give a damn about you." His life was miserable and he was intent on making his son's life miserable, too. When my friend started doing drugs and falling into all of the traps, I realized how easy it was to get caught up in those words.

Even at school, some of the teachers would tell me and all my friends, "Why should I care to help you? As soon as you get out of here all you're going to be is a criminal." I think about it today and it makes me sick. What kind of message is that? What future are you showing to these young kids? It was the typical negativity that cloaked my whole environment growing up. I watched those kinds of words sink so many people. I used them to fuel my fire.

I'll show you. I'm going to be somebody that people care about.

CHAPTER 6

The inviting red-brick towers and manicured green lawns—not a blade of grass out of place—made me feel like I had entered another world. The comparison to home was night-and-day. The trees that lined the campus—all sorts of different kinds, from magnolias to oak to sycamores and of course palm trees—were tall, healthy, and vibrant. And the garbage stayed in the trash cans, which weren't kicked over. The outer walls of the buildings were all bare, with no graffiti in sight. It was like I stepped onto the USC campus and into another world.

The students all seemed to drive nice cars. They dressed differently, they talked differently, they walked differently. Most everybody was white. Every day I found myself sitting in classrooms with people whose lives and whole identities were completely different than mine. My first two months at college I was still living with my parents in Compton, just twenty minutes or so down the 110. Once I settled into a room on campus, it became the best of both worlds: I was still their baby, but I had my independence and college life. I loved being close enough to have the option to go chill at home if I needed to, and I needed that safety net.

Being at USC was a culture shock. I'm not sure if I ever really got used to it. To this day, I still feel that way. I live in a nice house. When I travel, I stay in nice places. But it never feels normal. There's a reality of where I come from that forces you to be grounded. So many loved ones are still going through the same struggles today, and I can never look past that. So I don't take anything for granted. And I never feel far from home.

○   ○   ○

I was chilling on campus with Rome when I got a phone call from an old coach of mine from grade school named DeAndre. We had stayed in touch here or there over the years, and he was always supportive of me. He told me he was at USC that day and was hanging out at the library with his cousin, who he wanted me to meet. I brushed him off. "Maybe another time," I told him.

A few weeks later, I was in a hallway outside one of the practice courts at Galen Center, the school's massive athletic facility, when I spotted the equipment manager for USC's women's basketball team, Kiara Morrison, who was also a USC student. We had met a few times before, just small talk, but there was something about her that made me feel comfortable. It always felt natural, never forced. She had warm eyes and a smile that put me at ease. We started talking and she told me how her cousin was in the library trying to get me to come meet her. "Oh, *you're* DeAndre's cousin?" I didn't ask her out on a date that day, but we started hanging out more and more from then on—which was a challenge, because she kept herself so busy. She was locked-in on her schoolwork and I admired not only how ambitious she was but her incredible work ethic. It's a trait that's always drawn me to people—probably something that was instilled in me by my dad. I was blown away by Kiara, particularly her smarts. Her mom worked at USC in the Human Resources Department, and her dad had enjoyed a brief pro basketball career. Kiara was no slouch herself—she'd played two years at a smaller college before transferring to USC. Whether it was a difficult exam or any challenge placed in front of her, Kiara always had an incredible attention to detail and never took half-steps in anything she did. Some people—especially when you're as smart as she is—can easily coast by while doing the bare minimum. Not Kiara. She never took shortcuts, and that always stuck with me. I don't think she realizes how much of an impact that had on me, particularly at such a young age. No matter how much I accomplish in basketball, and regardless of how much my game improves each year, I always make sure to put in the work. And I give her credit for being one of the people that instilled that in me.

Kiara loved sports as much as I did. And she knew the intricacies of practically all of them. Whether it was a running route in football or an after-timeout possession in a basketball game, she could explain in detail the wheres and whys of everything. You could watch golf with her and she'd explain that the golfer's drive boomeranged far to the right because his hip was too open on his backswing. I don't know where she learned all of this, but she understood it all.

We never had a conversation about our relationship and what form it would take—I don't recall ever asking her "Do you want to go steady?" or anything like that—but we genuinely loved our time together. It just developed organically. Before you knew it, after my first and only year at USC, I got drafted and we were off to the NBA, together.

Her passion for sports has never waned. My earliest years in Toronto with the Raptors, she knew all of the team's plays and used to sit in the first row under the basket during every home game, calling out directions to my teammates and me like she was one of the coaches. There would be days when we'd be breaking down film after practice, watching segments from the previous game to see what worked and what didn't. The team's staff would come up to me all the time after editing the videos. "Kiara is all over our game tape, D." You could hear her clear as a bell.

◊   ◊   ◊

Kiara and I were watching the Beijing Olympics one day in August 2008, before my first semester at USC. There was Kobe, putting moves on his opponents—which I recognized as the same ones he had put on me during our training sessions earlier that summer.

Back in those days, my game was built on a foundation of pure athletic ability and a willingness to play hard, and it was enough to make a name for myself and earn a full-ride scholarship. But I was just raw talent with little refinement to my game. Basketball, at least at the level I aspired to reach, requires a sharp mind. You need to be able to read a defense—examining how your opponents are spacing the court, whether it's man-to-man coverage or a zone—while understanding exactly where each of your teammates is. It's about having a specific play to execute, and knowing exactly what adjustments to make based on what you see, going from Plan A to Plan B, C, D, or Z, depending on the situation. That took years for me to grasp. The athletics? That always came easily to me. I first dunked when I was eleven years old, in the sixth grade. If people were in my way, I could, and would, literally jump over them. At the college level—let alone in the NBA— I knew I wasn't going to be able to lean on what had gotten me to that point. It didn't take me long to realize that in Division One college hoops, *everybody* can jump out of the building and *everybody* plays hard—it was the only way to stay on the floor. All the players could do what had made me a special player growing up. I knew I couldn't get away with simply being a leaper anymore. I began to ask myself, *What's next?* thinking about elements of my game to work on, whether it was my handles, passing, and court vision, getting to the free-throw line, or studying the finer points of the game to boost my hoops IQ. I still ask myself the same question at the end of each season. For me to make it, I would need to evolve.

That wasn't the only thing that would have to change. Throughout high school I had worn number 23 in honor of Michael Jordan. But when I arrived at USC, there was a senior on the team who already wore that number. I didn't mind having to change it—LeBron James famously wore 23 for the Cleveland Cavaliers at the time and the number had become associated with him at that point. I had considered number 8, Kobe's jersey number during the first half of his Lakers career (before he switched it to 24 so it could be one higher than MJ's), but then I realized that I wanted a number that other superstars in the league weren't wearing. For the Beijing Games, Kobe had switched his jersey to number 10. The more I watched him tear up the Olympic competition that summer, the more it just seemed like a no-brainer. People always assumed I chose the number for the play on words with Compton—"Comp10," which later became the name of my apparel company. But that was just a nice coincidence. The real reason I wore number 10 was for Kobe.

I was expecting a major difference between the high school games I used to dominate and the caliber of play of the college game, and the NCAA delivered. But the speed and intricacies of the game were an adjustment for me. In my first three games I scored 24 points—total—as I got my footing. We had a good team at USC, anchored by our freshman center from Montenegro, Nikola Vučević, who would later become a teammate and good friend of mine in the NBA. Coming out of the gate, our team wasn't exactly lighting the basketball world on fire, but both I as a player and we as a team got better and better as the season wore on. By the time we reached the Pac-10 tournament at the end of the season in March, we were locked in and ended up winning the conference title. I was named tournament MVP. By then, I felt I had done enough to put myself on the radar of NBA scouts, and I was widely regarded as a top-ten pick if I left school to enter the draft. I thought about the promises I used to make my grandma when I was little, how I was going to take care of her and all her grandchildren, and the hours of blood, sweat, and tears I'd put in just to get this far. I knew I wasn't going to be returning to USC for a second year. As soon as the school year was over, I immediately shifted my focus to preparing for the NBA draft.

○   ○   ○

Oakland, California, reminded me of back home. I spent the summer after my college season there preparing for the 2009 NBA draft and my rookie season in the league with a trainer named Chris Farr—but everybody called him C-Farr. He was a former college coach, a member of Hall of Famer Jerry Tarkanian's staff at Fresno State in the nineties. Oakland was his city. "Here," he told me on one of my first days working with him, "we lock people up." He was referring to Gary Payton, aka "The Glove," a former pupil of his, one of the most tenacious defenders in NBA history and a proud Oakland native. C-Farr looked every bit like a former athlete. He was about six-two, barrel-chested with big shoulders, some extra padding around his gut, and a shaved head. His deep, booming voice commanded attention and respect. On the court he was a bulldog you weren't sure if you should pet or not. Off of it, he was approachable and made you feel like the center of the world.

I stayed in a one-bedroom condo in a rough part of downtown Oakland. When I first arrived I looked out the bedroom window and felt transported back to Compton. I saw the same type of struggle I'd witnessed my entire life. Poverty. Violence. Aggression. Anger. The air was thick with it, like I could reach out my hand and grab it. *Nah, this ain't the place.* The first time C-Farr took me there, he dropped me off, handed me the keys, and told me, "*Never* leave this condo." That was fine by me. I didn't care about going out anyway. I was just excited to be out of L.A.—it was the first time I'd left home to train and my first time away from home for any long stretch of time. Besides, this was a business trip.

When I did leave the condo it was to go to work. And C-Farr put me to *work*. In the mornings, he'd pick me up and we'd head to Merritt College, a community college nestled between Leona Canyon and Leona Heights Park, which overlooked the city. The workouts were the most intense I'd ever experienced—wind sprints while dribbling a ball in each hand with a weighted bungee cord tied around my waist for resistance; full-court games of one-on-one with a rotating cast of opponents, so they'd have fresh legs while I was struggling to stand; repeated drives into the paint, finishing at the rim through contact as C-Farr battered me like we were playing bumper cars with no padding (which brought me back to battling my dad on the Wilson Park courts back home). The colors of the blue-and-yellow stands appeared to blend together as the sweat poured down my forehead and into my eyes. In the afternoons, we'd drive to a beach and run in the sand for an hour (or longer) in one direction then an hour (or longer) back to the car. C-Farr was relentless and unforgiving. But everything was part of a bigger plan, some grand lesson.

I settled into a routine. Work out all day. Back to the condo. At night, I'd watch TV and crash out until the next morning. Rinse and repeat. On Friday night I would drive back to Compton, and return to Oakland by Monday morning.

For the first few weeks in Oakland, I had a training partner: Patty Mills, who was also preparing for the draft. Patty had moved from Australia to attend St. Mary's in Moraga, California. I was a projected top-ten draft pick, but Patty wasn't considered a top-ranked prospect; the stakes for him were even higher. In retrospect, Patty was the perfect person to train with. I'm not sure if he even knows it, but he pushed me incredibly hard in those days—and C-Farr will tell you that it was by design. What separated Patty from most anyone else was his motor. The dude just never stopped. I don't know if it was genetic, or an Australian thing, but he could run *all day*. On the beach runs he never slowed down and never even seemed tired. It made no sense. (A decade later we were teammates on the San Antonio Spurs—the NBA, you quickly learn, is a very small world—and I still hated any time I had to guard him in practice.) But with Patty running around like Forrest Gump it would keep me going. *I can't stop if Patty's still going strong,* I'd tell myself during those long runs.

"Have you ever been to the greyhound races?" C-Farr asked me one day on the way back from a particularly brutal run in the sand.

"No, can't say I have."

"Well, do you know how they keep the greyhounds going?"

I told him that I didn't, and he explained how the racetracks had plastic rabbits circling the inside of the track. The dogs weren't racing one another; they were chasing the rabbit. Patty, he implied, was that rabbit.

"You know," he said, "it's only when the greyhound reaches the rabbit that he realizes it isn't real. But, as you can see, Deebo, there's nothing fake about any of this, is there?" I understood what he was saying. To strive for greatness means you need to put in the work. The struggle is real. The work is real. There's no faking your way through any of this.

C-Farr and my dad got along well, and it wasn't long before he began to feel like a member of the family. They would talk often, Dad getting updates on my progress. One weekend, while I was back in Compton, I remember overhearing a conversation between them on the phone. "You keep pushing him," Dad told him. "My son has a lot more to give."

o o o

"Hey, isn't the car parked that way?" I pointed to the parking lot, which was disappearing farther into the distance behind C-Farr and me.

"Yeah, but I want to show you something," he told me, as we walked in the opposite direction of the lot following an exhausting morning workout session at Merritt College. We took a pathway that led to a winding staircase.

"Not much farther now," C-Farr said.

My legs were shot, but I followed, each step feeling like I was pulling my feet out of concrete. We reached the end of the staircase and found ourselves on top of a hill overlooking Oakland and the San Francisco Bay. I could see the flashes of light dancing off the ocean. The steady hum of freeway traffic below in the distance was interrupted every now and then by the calls of birds passing by overhead. We stood there, taking it all in, until C-Farr eventually broke the silence.

"Take a look down there," he gestured down toward the valley below. I recognized some of the buildings from the Oakland hoods where I was staying. There were clusters of apartments and row houses, run-down strip malls. "You can feel the heaviness from up here, can't you? You can feel the violence and the tension." He paused for dramatic effect, then went on.

"Down there is where we come from, and you can never forget your roots."

I nodded along, locked into whatever lesson C-Farr had in store for me on this hill.

"Now do you see across over there?"

He pointed out across the bay. I recognized the Golden Gate Bridge, which I had only seen before in movies. In the distance were the skyscrapers of downtown San Francisco, enormous, shiny, impressive, and totally foreign from where I grew up; I didn't need to use my imagination to picture the two different worlds in front of me.

"Over there, D, that's where basketball can take you," he said, his arms reaching out toward the bay. "The bright lights. The money and status. The success. The peace of mind . . . this game will make it all possible. But, DeMar, I want you to understand this: It's only possible if you're willing to put in the work."

PART TWO

CHAPTER 7

Bienvenue au Canada. Votre carte de déclaration douanière.

It was June 26, 2009, the morning after the NBA draft, and I was flying first thing on the ninety-minute trip from New York City to Toronto. My eyes were red and itchy from lack of sleep as I stared at the Canadian Border Services customs declaration card that travelers are required to fill out when entering the country.

What the hell? I thought. *"Bienvenue"? What is this, French?* I flipped the card over. In big, bold lettering it read: "Welcome to Canada." That's how I discovered that Canada, my new home for at least nine months of the year, is a bilingual country—and I didn't speak a word of French. The plane touched down on the tarmac at Toronto's sprawling Pearson International Airport. I took my first steps outside. The air felt hot and sticky from a recent thunderstorm—not really what I had expected. A member of the Toronto Raptors' front-office staff greeted me and led me to an SUV waiting to take me downtown, where I was scheduled to visit the arena and team facilities for the first time and do interviews with the Canadian media.

I settled into the back seat. As we maneuvered along the highway I noticed the road signs: *East/Est* and *West/Ouest* in both English and French. For the first time in the last twenty-four hours—the first time since my life changed forever—I thought: *What have I gotten myself into?*

Despite having never been to Toronto (or anywhere in Canada for that matter), from the beginning of the pre-draft process I felt a gravitation toward the Raptors. They were my first choice. They were the team I had hoped would select me on draft night.

I had met the team's general manager, Bryan Colangelo, and a handful of scouts and members of the team's front office staff once before, about a month before the draft, when they came to Oakland to watch me work out with C-Farr at Merritt College. Colangelo was like a character out of a movie. He wore fine, tailored suits with wide lapels and always had a dark tan, even while working in a winter climate like Canada. Like most hoops fans, I had known him as the architect of the Phoenix Suns during the Steve Nash era, and as the son of Jerry Colangelo, the former Suns owner and the head of the USA Basketball program. Among the Raptors contingent were Marc Eversley, a former Nike staffer who was making his way into the NBA, and Masai Ujiri, a former scout from Nigeria who had worked his way up the ranks quickly and had been named Toronto's assistant GM the year before. Both Marc and Masai would, for better or worse, play major roles in my career in the years to come.

I had already been working with C-Farr for weeks and weeks by the time the Raptors showed up. I was totally locked into our training regimen at that time and hyper-focused on preparing my mind and body for the next level. On the day the Raptors arrived I was *cooking*. A lot of teams came to watch me work out, and I felt like I had killed it in front of them all. I won't lie—it felt great to know I was putting myself in a position to leave a positive impression on all of these NBA personnel. It was a testament to how hard C-Farr and Patty and everybody was pushing me, and to how badly I wanted to make it. But my workout in front of Toronto was probably the best of them all. I was making shots from all over the floor and covering the court with ease. Thanks to our beach runs, my legs felt like they were spring-loaded; we would do our drill where I drive to the hoop while C-Farr does his Ray Lewis impression and basically tries to tackle me when I get into the paint. I would take the hit and absorb it, rise up, and finish with a nasty dunk. Everything I had experienced in my life to that point—death, loss, all the noise from people who told me I'd grow up to be nothing more than another jailed gangster in Compton—I channeled all of the rage it spawned inside me onto the court. The angrier I got, the more unstoppable I felt.

After the workout, I dropped into a folding chair, sweat pooling by my feet, and waited for my breathing to slow down and my lungs to fill with air. I knew I'd left a good impression, and of all the pre-draft workouts I'd done in front of NBA teams this was probably my best. The Raptors held the ninth pick in the draft, and, before he left the Merritt College gymnasium, Colangelo told me that if I was still available when they were on the clock, they were going to select me.

I was hyped. I didn't know anything about Toronto except that the CN Tower was there and, of course, it's where Vince Carter spent the first part of his career and put the city on the map in the NBA. Like every hooper my age, I grew up watching Carter. I was always a Kobe guy, but back in the early 2000s it was impossible not to be in awe of Vince, especially me being a leaper as well. There were a few years when I was a kid when, at the height of VC's power, the Raptors were contenders and he was one of the league's marquee stars. Their games used to air on national TV in America on Sundays at 1 P.M. Toronto time, which meant they were on at 10 A.M. back home in L.A. I remember going to Grandma's house on a Sunday morning to watch Carter battle Allen Iverson and the Philadelphia 76ers, scared to blink because I might miss another once-in-a-lifetime aerial move from the guy they called Half Man–Half Amazing. And then of course there was his performance at the 2000 dunk contest, which for my money is the most iconic of all time. My dad had that dunk contest on videotape and it was one of the most popular cassettes in the house. We watched that thing all the time, breaking down his dunks—the 360-degree reverse windmill, a between-the-legs alley-oop off the bounce, and, the showstopper, when Carter rises way above the rim and flies so high that he dunks his entire forearm into the basket, hanging off the rim with the crease of his elbow. I swear I damn near broke the tape rewinding it so much. It wasn't the actual dunks I was enamored with as much as the showmanship behind it all. There was a swagger he carried himself with that just leaped off the screen. He seemed perfectly aware that he was making history that night. He knew in the moment, even as he was still in the middle of it.

Just because Toronto had shown the most interest in me didn't mean that's where I would end up. Another team that was seriously considering drafting me was the Minnesota Timberwolves, who held pick numbers five and six. Two days before the draft they invited me to come to Minneapolis to work out and essentially said they would use one of their picks on me if I did. I didn't make the trip. I'm sure I would have been happy no matter where I went—the dream had always been to put on an NBA uniform, period—but at the time, the Timberwolves were the bottom of the barrel, and had barely cracked twenty wins in each of the past two seasons. Besides, there was just something about Toronto...

I arrived in New York City the night before the draft along with Mom, Dad, my cousin DeShaun, and my brother, Jermaine. Draft day itself was a whirlwind. I was doing media, signing autographs, getting a custom-tailored suit. *Is this what my life is now?* I thought. By the time the draft officially kicked off, I already kind of felt like I had made it. I was seated at a table with my family and my agent and began hearing the names come off the board. Blake Griffin was selected first overall by the Los Angeles Clippers, to the surprise of nobody. James Harden, who was also from L.A. and someone I had developed a friendship with after growing up competing against each other on the AAU circuit and attending basketball camps together over the years, went third overall. When it was time for Minnesota to make their first of two draft picks, I held my breath. With the fifth pick, they chose point guard Ricky Rubio, a teenage sensation from Spain, and then drafted another point guard, Jonny Flynn out of Syracuse, with number six. I exhaled. Next went Steph Curry at number seven to the Golden State Warriors, followed by forward Jordan Hill to the New York Knicks at number eight.

"With the ninth pick in the 2009 NBA draft..." As NBA commissioner David Stern began his announcement, I could see cameramen moving toward me and knew what was coming. "The Toronto Raptors select... DeMar DeRozan!" The cameras swarmed me and I was handed a hat with the Raptors claw logo on it. I hugged Dad first. Aside from me, nobody wanted this more for me than he did. That night was a celebration, and one of the first times I can remember seeing Dad cry.

I'd never had a passport before. Nobody in my family did, because there had never been a reason or opportunity to leave the country. I was lucky enough that I received mine the week of the draft, but being the only person with a passport meant that I was off to Toronto alone, leaving my circle back home. The next morning, as I boarded the plane to Toronto, reality set in. Not only was I leaving home—and really for the first time, given how close my college had been—but I was leaving the entire country, facing a new culture, new weather, new everything. A new life. I had put in the time and effort to be prepared for what basketball would be like at the next level. But looking back, I was completely unprepared for what was to come beyond hoopin'.

After I'd landed at Pearson, the SUV slowly made its way through the tail end of morning rush-hour traffic heading into downtown Toronto. After about half an hour, the city's skyline came into view. The closer we got, the bigger the skyscrapers grew as we approached the Air Canada Centre, which would become my office for the next nine years. The buildings were so tall it felt like they were reaching into space; it was all so much bigger than I expected. I felt my stomach and shoulders tense up, as my body mirrored my mind. I was nervous, fearful even. But I channeled that energy. Those nerves are a good sign, I told myself—it must mean there's something worth being nervous for.

Before meeting the media, I was shown around the facility. I saw the underground garage where the players parked (even though I didn't own a car), toured the locker room, and couldn't help but notice the framed Vince Carter photos on the walls. "Can we go see the court?" I asked at the first chance I got. I entered the tunnel into the empty arena and looked up into the stands, envisioning a sellout crowd of twenty thousand cheering their asses off, hopefully even wearing my jersey. The first time I played in front of a crowd that size was at the McDonald's high school All American Game the year before in 2008, which was held at the Bradley Center in Milwaukee where the Bucks used to play. I played well that night, and felt that the bigger crowd brought out the best in me. I remember just looking up into the crowd throughout that game thinking, *Damn, they play every game in front of crowds like this?* The same thought ran through my mind staring out into the Toronto court. *I'm about to be playing in places like this every night?!* It was beyond exciting, and I miss those moments now, when I was young and everything felt so new and electric. It's funny how you get used to this life. Don't get me wrong, it's always a cool feeling when you walk into the gym before tip-off and you see twenty thousand people there—it's been my world for nearly fifteen years now—but it's nothing like it was back when I was young and wide-eyed.

For my first two months in Toronto, I lived by myself out of the Westin Hotel in a room on the thirty-fifth floor that overlooked Lake Ontario, which looked so endless it might as well have been the ocean. The hotel was a stone's throw from the ferry terminal and just over a quarter-mile from the arena. Maybe it was because of my upbringing as an only child, but I didn't mind being alone. Truth is, it was a great thing for me at that time because it allowed me to home in and focus on being a pro. I locked into a routine immediately, spending most of my days at the arena going through drills and breaking down tape with the Raptors' training staff. I quickly developed a close bond with Eric Hughes, one of the assistant coaches, who I'm still close with to this day. Eric, who grew up in Oakland, was gearing up for his first season as an NBA coach after a couple years serving as a consultant for the Raptors' front office. Eric is a white guy and about twenty years older than me, but we hit it off from the jump. Who knows, maybe it was the California connection, but I think it's because we both wanted to succeed so badly and prove the team right for taking a chance on us. Eric was the one who checked in to make sure I was going to the gym every day and watching as much film as possible. Eric and I would learn the playbook together and talk about the differences between college and the NBA, where not only do you need to learn each play, but also four or five counters or adjustments you can make within that play, depending on how the defense reacts. I soaked in everything as best I could. I didn't know I could love it any more than I already did, but we were so immersed in hoops that we began to gain a different appreciation for the game.

Still, it was a grind and at times I felt like I was back in my apartment in Oakland preparing for the draft. With Kiara still taking classes to get her degree back at USC and my friends and family all back in L.A., I was just entirely consumed by basketball. It was all I knew.

I didn't know how to buy groceries (matter of fact I didn't cook) and didn't know about eating out at nice restaurants or anything like that. There was a small gyro stand outside the hotel lobby, and for dinner every night I would head down from my room and grab a gyro before heading back to the gym to put up shots.

Once I was done at the gym at night, I'd return to my hotel room and look out over Lake Ontario and be transported back home. I'd gaze up at the moon—the same one I used to stare at back home on the beaches, the same one Dad and I pointed up at in Vidalia all those years ago. *There's a whole world out there.*

Those first days in Toronto were lonely and tiring, but I never regretted any decision that led me to that place in time. From the moment I left college I understood that everything ahead of me would be different than anything I'd experienced before. Everything was new. I embraced it and promised myself that I would take it all in, whatever "it" was. I took that mindset to Toronto. *Nothing bad can come from this.* I repeated the phrase in my head like a mantra.

I looked down at a moonbeam reflecting across the water and took a deep breath. *Just take it all in.*

I was in Toronto, working my ass off in preparation for the start of my rookie season, but I still hadn't received an NBA paycheck. One day not too long after I'd arrived in the city, I made a cameo at a basketball camp about two hours outside Toronto. Afterward, I was handed a check for $5,000 for my appearance. I couldn't believe it. I called up Dad.

"I got a check for *five thousand dollars*! What am I supposed to do with it!?"

"OK, hold on to it for now," he told me. "I'll come and get the check and put it in your bank account for you."

The team was flying me out to Las Vegas the next week to work out with some of the other Raptors, so I made a plan to meet up with Dad in L.A. to give him the check and deposit it. I held on to that thing so tightly I was worried I'd smear the ink.

When I got back home, Dad retrieved the check and deposited it into my account. I still had the same starter Bank of America account that parents open up for their kids. It never had any money in it. I remember Dad proudly extending his arm to show me the receipt, and excitedly grabbing it from his hand and looking at the balance like, "Oh. My. *God*." I thought that shit was everything.

My rookie deal was for $1.9 million. "Surreal" doesn't begin to describe the feeling of coming from nothing and finding your way into that kind of money. Soon after I signed my first NBA contract, I got an advance of around $200,000 and, I promise you, I thought I was good for *life*. Literally forever. I asked my dad to look after my finances—there's nobody I trusted more than him—and told him that the first thing I wanted to do was buy a new house for him and Mom. They had done so much for me. They worked their asses off to put a roof over my head and built a protective circle around me that allowed me to escape the pitfalls of growing up in Compton. They deserved more than their lot in life, and I was dead set on providing that for them. Before the start of the season we looked at a handful of properties in Los Angeles and settled on a three-bedroom home in the View Park–Windsor Hills area, considered one of the more affluent Black neighborhoods in America, about twenty-five minutes northwest of Compton by car. Mom knew it was "the one" before we walked through the front door. But when I saw the price tag of the house my heart sank. It was listed at $800,000—four times the amount that I'd received from my advance. That's when I first learned about mortgages and how people finance homes. It was one of many moments in those days when I realized how much I had to learn.

Handing the key to that house over to Mom and Dad was one of the most dope feelings I've ever had. They were grateful, and proud as you can imagine. It felt like we were all starting over. But it was an adjustment. Whenever I asked how they were settling in, Dad would say, "It's just so quiet." The sirens. The gunfire. The helicopters. It's funny how you get used to it. It was like those noises were the soundtracks of our lives.

After I got my parents settled into their new home, I went to a car dealership in L.A. to treat myself. Those days of stealing Dad's ride in the middle of the night were in the rearview, and I wanted a car of my own so bad. I even knew exactly what I wanted: a black Cadillac Escalade. To me, that car was the ultimate symbol that I was on my way up in the world. I showed up to the dealership ready to do business. After learning about mortgages and understanding that you don't have to make big purchases like homes and cars up front in full, I decided to finance the car and brought a cashier's check for a down payment. I took the Escalade for a test ride, even though I'd already made up my mind, and sat down with one of the salespeople to finish the purchase. I pulled out my check and we got the paperwork started. There was just one problem: I didn't have a driver's license. But that's not what I told the salesperson. I said I just didn't have it on me and that I'd come back to the dealership with it after I bought the car. Nothing was going to stop me from leaving the lot with those wheels. The salesperson excused himself and disappeared into an office and returned a few minutes later.

"Don't worry about it," he said, as he took my check, "just get it to us when you get a chance."

I rode off the lot feeling like a king.

A couple days went by before the dealership called in a panic.

"You know we can get in trouble for this," the salesperson explained. "We can't lease you the car if you don't have a license."

A manager came on the phone and explained that legally I only needed a license to *lease* the car from the dealer. The only way I could keep the car without showing them a license, the manager explained, was if I bought the car outright. The cost was $76,000 plus tax. After putting a deposit on the house, and tucking some of my $200,000 advance into savings, that was money I flat-out didn't have yet. I was scrambling trying to find a solution, knowing that I couldn't afford the car and that my rookie season was around the corner and training camp was just a week or so away.

I kept the dealer waiting for a little longer—long enough to receive my license soon afterward, thanks to an expedited process—but the whole experience made me realize there was so much that I didn't know. *Everything* came with a learning curve in those days. Once the season got under way, that curve only got steeper.

The Raptors were coming off of a disappointing season when they drafted me in 2009. The team was just three years removed from winning the division for the first time since joining the NBA as an expansion franchise (along with the Vancouver Grizzlies) in 1995 and one season removed from making the playoffs, losing in the first round two years in a row. Just making the playoffs, period, was an accomplishment; winning had always been sporadic in Toronto. The team had only made it past the first round of the playoffs once, back in 2001 during the Vince Carter era. I was eleven.

In the 2008–2009 season, while I was at USC, the Raptors missed the playoffs entirely. The team won just thirty-two games and finished thirteenth out of fifteen teams in the Eastern Conference, despite a big year from Chris Bosh, the team's star. Three months into the season, Bryan Colangelo fired the head coach, Sam Mitchell, and replaced him with the team's lead assistant, Jay Triano, a Canadian who also coached Canada's national men's team. The next season, my rookie year, was his first full season as an NBA head coach. Jay was cool. You could tell that he was a young coach, trying to figure it out on the job. He really cared about not just winning but getting better, both as individuals and as a team. I couldn't ask for anything more. From the beginning of training camp, he was hard on me. Being a top-ten pick didn't mean a thing once you step between the lines. But I liked it that way. I didn't want to be coddled and feel all comfy now that I was in the pros, you know? From my dad to C-Farr, I always responded to being pushed. I worked hard to do everything that was asked of me and was determined to be a sponge, just like the kid sitting in the front row of Kobe's basketball camp, soaking in every word. One of the assistant coaches on Triano's staff was Alex English, the former Denver Nuggets star whose game tapes I watched repeatedly with Dad growing up (here's some NBA trivia for you: During the entire decade of the eighties, no player scored more total points than my guy Alex English).

My first year, our team was a mix of veterans and younger players. There were a handful of teammates who had been on the

Raptors squads that appeared in the playoffs in recent years, like Rasho Nesterović, who'd won a title with the San Antonio Spurs, where he spent most of his career; José Calderón, a hyper-competitive point guard from Spain entering his fourth NBA season after an established pro career in Europe; and Bosh, who had been named to the All-Star team every year since 2006 and was entering the last year of his contract when I arrived. One of the veterans who really took me under his wing in those early days was Jarrett Jack, our backup point guard, who was in his first season with the team and is now an assistant coach with the Detroit Pistons. Jack was all business—he was one of those guys who didn't speak too often, but when he did, you listened. He took it upon himself to show me the ropes and was always pulling me aside during practices or whenever, pointing out things like why you should get to the arena extra-early on game days—especially on the road, so you can get a feel for the dimensions of the arena—and the importance of learning how to sleep on the team plane.

I was at a different stage in life than most of my teammates. I was a kid, wide-eyed and embracing one new experience after another. They were grown-ass men, with families they'd go home to after practices or games.

The only other players close to me in age were Sonny Weems and Amir Johnson, and they quickly became my closest teammates. Amir was an L.A. kid like me who went to high school in Westchester, near Inglewood, about twenty-five minutes east of Compton. He had been drafted straight out of high school by the Detroit Pistons before being dealt to Toronto. Sonny was a second-round draft pick who played one season in Denver before being traded to Toronto a month or so after I was drafted. He was super-talented and could do a bit of everything. He and I had killer chemistry on and off the court, and I'd envisioned us playing for years together, running the wings for the Raptors.

We spent so much time together, exploring the city—Mississauga, Scarborough, all the Toronto boroughs—and goofing around with fans. It gave us something to do while the rest of our teammates were busy with their families. The thing about day-to-day life in the NBA is that there is so much downtime. On an off-day, you might practice at 10 or 11 in the morning. After practice ended, I usually stuck around to do some weightlifting or put in some extra work, and then the rest of the day is at your disposal. (More often than not I'd make my way back to the gym late at night to work on my shooting.) On a game day, you'll go to the arena for the morning shootaround—a long-standing tradition in the league, where teams gather on the court and get a light practice in and maybe go over the game plan for that night. (On the road, the shootaround can also help you get a feel for the arena's dimensions and sightlines to the basket, which are slightly different in every NBA arena, depending on how the seating is laid out.) Then you have the whole day to kill before heading back to the court an hour or two before tip-off.

When we were at practice or preparing for games, we took our jobs very seriously, taking a cue from the veterans around us. Our approach to the game was so workmanlike that we craved any chance to just be the twenty-year-old kids that we were. These days, I see young players in the league spending all of their free time in their hotel rooms, playing video games. Don't get me wrong, I've done some serious damage in "Madden" in my day, but that wasn't really our thing. This was when social media was really taking off and we were all really active on Twitter. I loved interacting with the fans on there. At the beginning of the season, the team handed each player this book filled with tickets for our home games for us to give to friends and family. I would write stuff like "Meet us at Best Buy for tickets to the game." We'd hit up the Best Buy in downtown Toronto, a few blocks from the Air Canada Centre, and there'd be a shitload of people waiting for us wanting tickets. Other times, one of us would write that we were going to hit up some gym thirty minutes outside the city and play pickup with any fans that showed up. One of our favorite places to hit up was an amusement park north of the city called Canada's Wonderland. It reminded me of Knott's Berry Farm back in California, where my dad used to take me and my cousin Kevin when we were kids. At Canada's Wonderland people would recognize us but they were cool—it's one of the great things about the Canadian fans. Fans knew we were just looking to have fun just like them. Sonny, Amir, and I spent so much time together that the media even gave our group a nickname: "The Young Onez" or "Young Gunz."

In November, early in the season, we had just returned to Toronto from a short but taxing road trip—three games in four nights—that took us from New Orleans to Dallas to San Antonio. Coach Triano had put me in the starting lineup, but I wasn't exactly lighting the league on fire. In high school and even at USC, I'd had the green light to shoot more or less whenever I wanted and was used to the offense flowing through me. Now in the NBA, I was suddenly a fourth option at best. On the road trip I scored 8 points *total*. I think I took five shots over the entire three games. Maybe Jack could sense that I was feeling some type of way: The day after we landed in Toronto was an off-day, and he invited me over for dinner at the house he and his family were renting. Jack had his own private chef, which was mind-blowing to me at the time, but I've since learned is pretty commonplace in the league—especially for veteran players who figure out that, as you age, what you eat can play a big role in keeping in shape and extending your career. I remember sitting down at the table, and the chef set a plate in front of me. I didn't know what I was looking at. It looked like sawdust.

"What the hell is this?" I asked Jack.

"Man, c'mon, eat your damn food," he shot back.

"No, but seriously, what *is* this?"

"It's couscous," he told me. "Dig in."

I scooped a handful of the fluffy sawdust onto my fork, exhaled, and shoveled it into my mouth. It was *amazing*. *Man*, I thought, *one day I gotta get me a chef.*

I was just a young guy trying to make it. So whenever and however I could be around established guys like Chris and the veterans, I jumped at the opportunity. They'd ask me to go get doughnuts for the locker room, typical rookie hazing stuff, but every now and then they'd let me hang with them away from the court. Anytime I was around the older guys on the team, it made me feel like a square peg trying to fit into a round hole. We would go out to a restaurant and I would be scanning the menu for chicken tenders or some wings. Meanwhile, they're ordering real meals—choosing the perfect side dishes to make sure they get a healthy balance of starches and greens, and letting the waiter know precisely how they want their steak cooked. I took notes.

As much as I had to learn away from basketball, the learning curve on the court was even sharper. I played shooting guard, and at the time it was the most stacked position. In any given game I'm matching up with all-stars like Dwyane Wade, Brandon Roy, Ray Allen, Joe Johnson, Vince Carter—and obviously Kobe. Each game blended together like one long "Welcome to the NBA" moment. Trying to keep up with those guys took everything out of me. After a night chasing B-Roy or D-Wade around the court, my legs felt like they were set in concrete. It was a tired I'd never felt before. And it happened night after night.

Now that I'm older, I know what it's like to match up with a rookie or young player. It's hard to describe, but there are times when you step onto the court and see your matchup across from you in the flesh and you can just *know* you have the advantage.

They look like easy prey, like I'm about to eat them for lunch—and that's exactly how those guys were looking at me. There was one game against Detroit where I drew the matchup with Richard "Rip" Hamilton, a shifty scorer and one of the key players on the Pistons' championship team in '05. A few years removed from his prime, he was still a pain in the ass to guard. On the first play of the game, as we crossed half-court he called out to his teammates: "Young fella guarding me!"

He faked one way—I bit—and darted in another and then disappeared behind a screen. "We got a fish out of water here!" he yelled, catching a pass mid-stride as he pulled up for an easy jump shot that swished through the net.

○ ○ ○

By March 25, with less than one month until the end of the regular season, I was feeling good about my rookie year. Our team was competitive, and I'd been in the starting lineup of every game I played since opening night. I was making real strides, too, averaging double-digit scoring so far during the month of March. So when one of our coaches pulled me aside after practice and told me that I was being removed from the starting lineup, that shit crushed me.

"Why?" I asked. "What did I do wrong?"

Back then, I used to think it was the head coach who made all the decisions. Eventually you learn that there are so many off-court factors that go into on-court decisions. The reality is, in the NBA, most coaches are following a higher power: the front office.

I was getting angrier and could feel the blood rushing to my head. "I'm doing everything that's being asked of me." I left without saying another word to anybody. When I got home I shut my phone down and tried to wrap my head around what had happened. I couldn't understand it. I'd been a starter on every team I've been on for my entire life. Even coming to the NBA, the highest level of basketball on the planet, hadn't changed that. So why now?

The next night against the Denver Nuggets, I arrived at the Air Canada Centre still confused and pissed off, but I tried not to show it. In the locker room I kept to myself, still not talking to anybody and processing my emotions. I ended up scoring 15 points, missing just one shot the whole night, in a 1-point loss. It was one of my better games of the season, but I couldn't help but feel embarrassed. Most jobs, if you get demoted, nobody outside of your workplace knows about it. But as I watched the opening tip-off from my new, unfamiliar seat on the bench I felt like the whole world was watching me. After the game ended, they were talking about my demotion on TV, how I wasn't good enough for a starter role and compared me to other guys from my draft class. I was so mad. That night, I called home. I think I just needed to hear my mom tell me everything was going to be all right.

At the time, we were one game below .500 at 35–36, and holding on tightly to the eighth and final playoff spot in the Eastern conference. The stakes were high. Bosh, our best player, was in the last year of a three-year deal he'd signed in 2007. Picked fourth by Toronto in the famous 2003 draft that also included LeBron James and D-Wade, he'd spent his whole career up to that point with the Raptors. He was the franchise player, at the time the leading scorer in team history. His contract situation quietly hung over that season: Will he stay or go?

In the meantime, as the season wound down, I found out that the team was beginning to sense that Chris wasn't going to re-sign. The writing was on the wall: He wasn't coming back. I had directed most of my anger and frustration at the coaching staff. Turns out, word had come from Bryan Colangelo and the front office to bench me for Antoine Wright, a twenty-six-year-old vet who had been around the league. The Raptors' brass felt that the team would have a better chance to win if we didn't have to put as much time toward developing the young kid. A few games later the Clippers were in Toronto to play us. I had met one of their star players, Corey Maggette, a bunch of times back in L.A. when I was in high school. He was one of the guys my uncle Chico Brown would take me around to meet, and Maggette was always willing to offer advice. During a stoppage in play, as we were walking back to the Clippers bench, he grabbed me by my waist with his tree-trunk arms.

"Keep your head up, stay professional, and stay locked in," he told me. "Shit like this happens—you better not let it break your confidence." I took it to heart and played some of my best ball of the season down the stretch coming off the bench, including my only 20-point performance of the year.

One week after that Clippers game, with six games left on the schedule, we were playing in Cleveland and Chris Bosh caught an accidental elbow to the face that broke his nose and part of his upper jaw just three minutes into the game. You could tell he was shook. He left the court clutching his face. He didn't suit up for the rest of the season. We ended up missing the playoffs.

That summer, Chris left Toronto to join LeBron and Wade on the Miami Heat.

CHAPTER 8

I was back in L.A. during the summer after my rookie year, crashing at Mom and Dad's new place in View Park. C-Farr and I were back into our training routine, two workouts a day plus a shootaround, when I heard the news that Chris had decided to take his talents to South Beach.

I kept reading stories saying the Raptors couldn't win now with him gone, how there was no go-to player on the roster. I thought about getting benched at the end of the season. My temples began to hurt. I grabbed my phone and wrote a post on Twitter and hit send: "Don't worry, I got us . . ."

The fans rallied around the message, but I wrote it as much as motivation for myself as them. I was just coming off my rookie year and I had my moments, but I hadn't exactly torn the roof off the joint. You have to realize that at every other point in my life I'd always been basically the best player on the court. The medals and trophies used to pile up in my room back home, mementos from different tournaments and leagues. My rookie year there was none of that. And I hated it. I remember at All-Star weekend in Dallas I was asked to compete in a "dunk-off" against Eric Gordon on Friday night at halftime of the annual Rookie-Sophomore game. I nearly turned it down when I found out I hadn't made the roster for the rookie team. So I watched the first half on a monitor in the concourse as I waited, *knowing* I could compete out there. On the screen I saw James Harden, who I'd shared the court with countless times rising through the ranks in L.A., dribbling through the other team. I watched Brandon Jennings, who traveled with me and my dad from Compton to the McDonald's high-school All American Game in Milwaukee two years earlier, hit a shot from the same spot I'd seen him hit it a million times before when we were growing up. There were also plenty of dudes who you'd never hear from again in the league.

When Gordon came onto the court for the dunk-off, sweating through his jersey from playing in the first half, I was embarrassed. I channeled it, won the dunk-off, and made it to the finals of the dunk contest the next night. Normally it'd be a huge deal for me—think of the hours Dad and I spent watching tapes of old contests—but I was still too frustrated about the rookie-game snub to enjoy any of it.

At the end of the season I looked for motivation in any form I could get and added Chris's departure to the list. Plus, I knew what the Toronto fans had been through in the past. They loved Vince Carter to death, and when he asked to be traded I think it hurt them. Now, I just watched their best player leave again. *Well, I wanted them to know, I'm not leaving. I'm here, Toronto, and we're going to turn this around together.* As soon as I hit send it lit a fire under me. I spent that summer training like crazy, thinking, *We're about to surprise 'em all. I'm going to bust my ass to make sure we get into the playoffs next season.*

Don't worry, I got us . . .

I pinned the tweet to the top of my profile page. It stayed there for the next eight years.

I meant what I had written. I was ready to step up and do what I could to carry the torch from Chris and take the franchise further than it's ever been. But, man, was I ever naïve. As far as the Raptors' front office was concerned, heading into my second season, the team was starting over. It was like when Chris left our whole mission changed. The entire situation turned on a dime. We were just fighting for a spot in the playoffs and now suddenly we're rebuilding completely. The business of the NBA, I was learning, can be ruthless.

° ° °

Sonny and I only ended up playing one more season together in Toronto, and it was one to forget. In my second year we were terrible. Just fucking awful. We won twenty-two games, good for second-to-last in the conference. It was the team's lowest win total in sixteen years—since the Raptors' inaugural year in the NBA in 1995. In the off-season, Sonny was a free agent and the team let him walk. That same summer, 2011, the NBA had a lockout as negotiations with the players' union stalled, pushing back the start of the next season. Instead of waiting, Sonny ended up signing with a team in Russia and didn't return to the NBA for four more years. It hurt watching him leave. He was my closest teammate. I felt like we had the makings of a dynamic duo on the court and would be playing together our whole careers. We thought we were going to grow together as players and people, but I learned the hard way that the pro leagues don't work like that.

As much as I hated losing, there was no doubt that my training with C-Farr was getting results. My game improved quickly as I got more accustomed to the speed and power of the NBA game. I went from averaging 8 points a game as a rookie to more than 17 in my second year. After one stretch when I scored 30 points in back-to-back games, I got a text from Kobe telling me that all my hard work was beginning to show—and not to get comfortable. It was like my dad always told me: "You have more to give."

That summer, in 2011, Bryan Colangelo fired Triano and replaced him with Dwane Casey, who had just won the championship as an assistant coach with the Dallas Mavericks. It was Casey's defensive schemes that helped Dallas and Dirk Nowitzki contain the Miami Heat and LeBron, Wade, and Bosh.

He'd been coaching in the NBA since the early nineties, including on those iconic Seattle SuperSonics teams starring Gary Payton and Shawn Kemp. Dwane was definitely what you would call old-school. He grew up in rural Kentucky and had a hint of a southern drawl to prove it, and had worked in the tobacco fields when he was a kid.

As a team we were looking for any type of hope and direction, a light to walk toward. That's what Casey represented. When he arrived, it was a chance for us to get away from that helpless feeling of losing, and I was excited to work with a coach who had played a role in the development of players like Payton and Nowitzki.

As a coach he didn't accept excuses and was the kind of person you wanted to push yourself for and compete. He reminded me a lot of my dad in that way. Casey came into training camp real militant. He preached hard work, toughness, and structure, and worked to build some type of identity for our team. Before the season started, Casey had a giant slab of stone placed inside our locker room, right when you enter the door. "Pound the rock" became a slogan he used all the time. When we entered the locker room we were supposed to press our fist against the rock—"pound the rock to get better," Casey would say. It was something he heard coach Gregg Popovich had done with the San Antonio Spurs during one of their many title runs. It was a gimmick, and maybe a little corny, but we were all for it. Anything for change.

We competed hard for Casey from the jump, but that third year was a struggle nonetheless. As my role on the team grew, I started to understand the dynamics of a professional basketball team. The pressure that travels from top to bottom. From the general manager to the equipment manager, in the NBA everybody is just working to keep their job. I felt that pressure as much as anybody. As a player, the success of everybody in the organization hinges on you and your performance. I won't lie: Once I realized that, everything became more of a grind. I read everything being said about us. How if the new coach couldn't turn things around, the problem must be the players. Meanwhile, I'm looking around the league and watching James Harden playing in the Finals with the Oklahoma City Thunder, or Steph Curry on the rise with the Golden State Warriors. They're going on deep playoff runs and commanding respect around the league. I started having trouble sleeping again. When I was younger, I would lie in bed awake, eyes wide open as the sounds of the night burst through my window. But these days I would say goodnight to Kiara, who understood I was trying to process it all, and just stay up by myself keeping busy. Watching movies, scrolling social media. Keeping my mind as occupied, or distracted, as possible.

When you're on a losing team, players come and go as the front office is constantly retooling the roster. Suddenly, every year that goes by you have six, seven, eight new teammates. I began to accept that the guy sitting next to me in the locker room might not be there the next season—in fact, there was a better chance of him being gone than the other way around. That was just the norm. Losing a teammate is nothing like losing a life, but it was honestly hard not to think about Davian and the friends and family I'd lost growing up back in Compton. It was hard not to think about the faces fading in the *Back to the Future* photos that always haunted me. Here I am in an entirely new chapter in my life, seemingly on top of the world. Yet here I am, powerless, watching more people fade from my life with each year. It was the same thing I'd dealt with as a kid.

The revolving door is a reality in the NBA. Once I realized that, I told myself I wouldn't make the mistake I'd made with Sonny again—that I wouldn't get attached to teammates like that. I began to look at being an NBA player less as a joy, an outlet like hoops had always been for me, and more as an occupation. Don't get me wrong, I still obsessed over my work, but it was just that: work. I felt I needed to be distant in order to avoid getting hurt. To be honest, it wasn't hard. I'd had a lot of practice in not allowing others to get close to me, or vice versa. I looked at teammates like, "All right, we're here to do a job, right? You do your job the best you can and I'll do mine the best I can, and that's all that matters." Soon I didn't care about anything else, including whether teammates or coaches came back or not. I'd felt too much pain losing people close to me before. You're damn right I was going to protect myself from having to feel that hurt again.

○   ○   ○

I get why people assume that, as pro athletes, we're really close with all of our teammates. We spend so much time with one another—more than with our own families—and are always traveling together. But it ain't like that. Sometimes you can go the whole season without saying a word to some of the people you spend the most time around.

In the summer of 2012 the team made a trade that brought in

Kyle Lowry. Although he was a star player in college at Villanova in his hometown of Philadelphia, Kyle's NBA career to that point had been pretty rocky. He'd been traded twice already after being drafted in the first round by Memphis in 2006. There were rumors that he clashed with coaches at his previous stops. He landed in Toronto with one year left on his contract and zero intent on staying with the Raptors once the season was through—he'd made that pretty obvious to us all.

My immediate impression? I thought he was kind of a dickhead. Kyle was always on his own time. He'd come and go and never really seemed a part of the team. He walked around the facility in a hoodie with the hood pulled up over his head and always seemed short-tempered with *everybody*. While I would stay late at practice, talking with coaches, putting up shots or getting in some extra work, he would make a beeline to the exit as soon as practice wrapped. I used to look at him like *Man, what the fuck is this guy's problem?* Meantime in his head, he's thinking *I'm out of here the first chance I get.* Toronto was nothing more than a stopover for him.

Being young and coming from the environment I was raised in, I was so single-minded and thought that if somebody acted differently, they were weird. I really thought that if you weren't exactly like me, I couldn't relate to you. Kyle and I were both guarded for our own reasons. That whole season, we didn't say a word to each other off the court.

When I look back at it now, I realize that Kyle was on his shit from the moment he arrived. He'd come into work early and busted his ass—almost always in a full sweat already by the time the rest of us got to the gym—and took care of his business. As soon as practice, or a game, was over, he was out of there. Kyle was treating the NBA like the cutthroat business it is. He knew this wasn't a social club—this was our livelihood. Eventually I came to respect that.

Fact is, he was a killer point guard and knew how to command a team on both sides of the floor. But he's a guy who wears his heart on his sleeve, no matter how it might make you feel. His bullshit detector is always running, and that can rub people the wrong way—especially if you don't understand where he's coming from. We were just such opposites. He was eyeing his exit from the moment he arrived, but I was fiercely loyal and preparing to commit to the Raptors organization long-term.

The day before Halloween, on the eve of the 2012–13 regular season, I signed a four-year, $38-million contract extension. I saw the deal as another stepping stone. What blew my mind as much as the money was what that contract represented. I mean, yeah, it made me feel validated for the work I'd put in, but more than anything else—the wealth, the status—the contract gave me motivation to prove that I was worth every penny. I entered the season wanting to show exactly why I received that extension, and sure enough, I had the best year of my career to that point.

There was never any doubt in my mind that I would return to Toronto—I hadn't even considered another option. I was loyal to a city and organization that had taken me in with open arms. While the team still had a long way to go to becoming competitive, I was in a good place in the city. Kiara and I settled into a condo right next to the Air Canada Centre. From our spot on the fortieth floor, we overlooked Maple Leaf Square—what they now call "Jurassic Park." The setup worked for us. The apartment overlooked Lake Ontario, so I was able to see the moon clearly at night. And being literally next door to my office was obviously a perk. So many nights I would pop over on a whim—sometimes there'd be a concert going on, or a hockey game—and I'd just walk through the crowds and into the practice gym to get some shots up. We usually had family, like my cousin DeShaun, stay with us. Because of Mom's lupus, it was a bit more difficult for her to travel back and forth. When I was still in high school, she began complaining about worsening pain in her joints. The colder the weather got, the worse her pain would become. Next thing I know, I started noticing red dots appear on her hands. I didn't know it then, but I've since learned that the spots were a telltale sign of lupus. Early in my career I arranged for her to get the best care possible at home, helping to make sure Mom was eating right and taking the proper medication. I became an official ambassador with Lupus Canada, a national charitable foundation based out of Toronto, and quickly realized that just by sharing my own personal experience caring for a family member with lupus that I could help others. Still, despite it all, Mom and Dad would visit me in Canada whenever they could.

Kiara and I were shopping for furniture for our condo ahead of the season when she dropped a bomb on me: "I'm pregnant."

She waited a few beats. I was stunned and silent.

"Well, aren't you going to say something?"

My face was blank while I tried to process what she just said. We were both so young, twenty-two years old, and felt like we were just kids ourselves. Shit, I still lived with my parents when I went back home! We waited a couple of months before we told anybody, just took time between the two of us to sit with the news. It was a lot to take in. Basketball had been my life to that point. It was all-consuming, and had been for practically as long as I could form coherent memories. My whole world was about to change and I didn't know how I was going to navigate it.

As a team, the Raptors were terrible that year. Kiara's due date was in May, and I remember at one point in the season thinking: "Damn, I'm going to be a father before I even play in a playoff game." I was continuing to make strides in my game and finished the season as a top-twenty scorer. But after three years of losing, you could tell the front office was under a ton of pressure to make something happen. It led to us trading for Rudy Gay, an all-star talent at small forward. I was jacked when we brought in Rudy—we'd forged a friendship during a trip to China for a Nike event right after my rookie year. We hung out together the entire time, and remain tight to this day (fun fact: Our birthdays are one week apart). I loved having him as a teammate, but we just weren't able to translate our chemistry to winning basketball.

As soon as the season wrapped up, Kiara and I were back in Los Angeles, waiting for our daughter to arrive. On May 10, with the due date around the corner, we went to the hospital for a routine checkup—or so I thought. Soon after we arrived at the maternity ward, one of the doctors told us we wouldn't be leaving until the baby came. I was terrified and felt helpless. It was another day and a half until Diar arrived. In the delivery room, a nurse handed the baby to me. I held her in my arms and then against my chest. It was love at first sight, and I could feel my whole universe shifting. And I'd never been more proud of anyone than I was of Kiara in that moment.

We were just like any other nervous new parents. After staying an extra day at the hospital, I drove my girls home, hands on the wheel at ten and two the entire time.

I never wanted to be away from my baby. I carried her everywhere, nestled into the crook of my elbow on my shooting arm. We were inseparable, and I didn't know how I was going to go through an entire season of being back-and-forth from the road for eight months of the year. Diar was about three months old the first time I left her for the night. I was invited to a friend's bachelor-party weekend—four days in Miami. Thirty-six hours into the trip I booked a flight and came back home.

Diar is a lot like her dad. She's quiet and keeps to herself, especially if she doesn't know you. And she's stubborn. If she wants to do something, she won't stop until she figures it out. She gets a lot of that obsessive behavior from me. When she was five or six, we got her a Rubik's Cube, and she wanted to figure it out so badly. She'd be playing with us and then all of a sudden disappear into her room to work on it, and sure enough, she figured it out on her own. I never would have guessed how dope it is to watch a person come into their own. But it's the greatest. She's really into animals—especially ocean creatures—and she says she might want to be a zoologist. But she's also really into earth and space, so maybe she'll be an astronomer. I just tell her that you can accomplish whatever you want.

One of my greatest pleasures was seeing the effect that Diar had on my dad. He was such a softie around her. I had never seen him like that. It was like Diar stripped all the armor off him. Fatherhood brought out a softer side in me, too. I was grateful. Being with my girls helped me access a part of me that I hadn't had much chance to tap into before. Growing up, the only way to get by was by being hard and having a stronger shield than the next man. There was so much devastation that it was the only way to keep moving forward without becoming another casualty of the streets. When I held Diar, the only thing I wanted her to feel was love.

○ ○ ○

The revolving door never seemed to stop in Toronto. A few months after Diar was born, the team got rid of Bryan Colangelo and named Masai Ujiri as team president and general manager. I had first met Masai during my pre-draft workout for the Raptors, and he was one of the people that advised the team to select me. Back then, Masai was a quiet guy who operated behind the scenes. The Denver Nuggets hired him away from us and promoted him to GM. He returned to Toronto after being named Executive of the Year the season before and was given the job of rebuilding the team from the bottom up.

I had dinner with him before the season at a steakhouse in Las Vegas, and I saw a noticeable change since I'd first met him. Gone was the shy, reserved guy. Now he was cool and confident. It felt like even his handshake had become firmer during his years away. Masai laid out his plan to me: He was going to clear the shop and get rid of everybody he didn't bring in himself. The Rudy situation, he added, wasn't working. It had been a last-ditch effort by the previous regime to team me up with a star player, and Masai had deemed it a total failure.

We were back in Los Angeles for a game against the Lakers in early December. It was a big night for Laker fans: the return of Kobe Bryant. Eight months earlier, with two games left in the previous season, Kobe had ruptured his Achilles tendon. For a hooper, who spends an entire game planting, pivoting, and pressing off the balls of their feet, it's one of the most devastating injuries there is. It can be a career death sentence. So, of course, Kobe is only out *eight months* before suiting up again. Now he was making his season debut against us, and the whole world was watching him. But I was too distracted to pay that any mind.

The afternoon before the game, I was chilling with my folks at their house before we all headed to the Staples Center when Rudy called.

"Deebo, it's done," he told me. "They just traded me to Sacramento."

As tough as it was to see him go, at least I had seen it coming. We'd lost five in a row and were 6–12 to start the season. Rudy was the first domino to fall. I thought I was next. I kept to myself once

I got to the arena. I stayed quiet, like I always do when I'm trying to process what's going on around me. I hated not having control over my future. I hated being treated like I was dispensable. I hated losing.

I've never been the most vocal guy in the locker room. On our team, Kyle, who'd decided to stick around Toronto for a while longer, was becoming the biggest voice (and I don't mean the loudest, but he was that, too). But in private moments, I began taking more of a leadership role. On the court I was our go-to player by then, and that came with responsibilities. In the visitors' locker room at Staples Center before tip-off, just after our coaches had left and it was just us players, I stood up.

"Fuck them all," I said. "Fuck what outside people got to say. Fuck what upstairs got to say." Everybody's heads began nodding. "We in this together."

We jumped out to a 10-point lead in the first quarter and barely looked back. I dropped 26 points, Kyle added 23, and Amir went off for 32 points. And we got the win.

We weren't celebrating or nothing—the writing was already on the wall. The flight back to Toronto that night was quiet, just the white noise of the airplane cabin. We all figured that once we landed, the rest of the pieces would begin to fall.

Our team had been left for dead—we were blowing it up and everybody knew it. That was literally the plan. Masai was blunt about it. He was straight up with us and said that I, Kyle, and everybody else on the roster was on the trading block and likely to be dealt. "It's only a matter of time," he said, adding that he'd try to see if he could help us out if there was a specific team we wanted to go to. I didn't want to go nowhere. I wanted to stay in Toronto. It's why I signed the extension and why Kiara and I put our roots down raising our newborn in the city.

The management was on the verge of sending Kyle to the New

York Knicks, but the deal fell apart at the last minute. Then they were preparing a trade to send me to a Western Conference team, I think it was Golden State. It was practically a done deal—at least that's how it was presented to me.

A few days before Christmas, we headed out on a four-game road trip. The holidays are always a tough time of year for NBA players. We're almost always traveling and away from our families. It crushed me to be away from Diar with her very first Christmas around the corner.

Our first stop was Dallas, and I remember having a conversation with the guys on the plane. "Look, man, we're gonna sink or swim right now. Whatever is gonna happen is gonna happen. They say we're out? Well, let's at least go out fighting." We landed in Dallas and beat the Mavericks by one. Then it was on to Oklahoma City to play the first-place Thunder. Another win. We went 3–1 on the road trip playing solid team basketball. We were sharing the ball and getting contributions from everybody. Kyle and I were playing off each other well and figuring out how our games could complement each other. He knew where to find me in my spots and I learned to recognize when he had a hot shooting hand and when he needed relief.

After that trip, Masai decided he was going to give us a little more time. Another week. That week turned into a month. We won eight out of our next ten games. By then, we'd forced their hand. We were going to ride it out for the rest of the year.

CHAPTER 9

6.2 seconds.

It's Game 7. We're about to inbound the ball down by one with a chance to advance to the second round of the 2014 playoffs. The sellout Air Canada Centre crowd is a sea of red and white cheering us on. We'd drawn a first round matchup with the Brooklyn Nets, who had some serious veteran talent—Joe Johnson, Deron Williams, Kevin Garnett, and Paul Pierce. But those OGs couldn't call me a fish out of water anymore.

That season I was named to my first NBA All-Star team. I remember lacing up my kicks in the locker room in New Orleans, my stall right next to guys like LeBron, D-Wade, Melo. There was a dominating presence about them that really stood out to me. They just owned the room. But they made me feel like the respect I had for them was mutual. That mattered to me. I had put in so much effort to make sure that I belonged at that level. I never partied. I never hung out at clubs. For my first few years in the NBA, I didn't take a vacation—I felt like I just didn't deserve one until I accomplished something in the league.

Nobody expected us to make the playoffs, never mind grab home-court advantage. After we traded Rudy, we were supposed to have a fire sale. Instead, we surprised everybody and closed out the season strong. The whole city was buzzing like I'd never seen before. Normally it was all about hockey and the Toronto Maple Leafs, but suddenly I couldn't pick up a take-out meal without people coming up to me chanting, "We the North!"—the branding slogan the team put out in time for the playoffs. The fans were wild. They were starved for a competitive team to root for. It was like we'd woken up a sleeping giant. And nobody wanted this run to end.

6.2 seconds. The referee blew his whistle and I cut toward the sidelines to receive a pass, but I'm covered. Time for plan B. The ball finds its way to Kyle at the top of the key. *4.2 seconds.* He crosses over to the middle of the court and is swarmed by three Nets defenders at the top of the arc. *2.8 seconds.* Kyle pushes the ball forward and lunges between Garnett and Williams toward a waiting Paul Pierce. *1.1 seconds.* In one motion he reaches down, collects the ball off the bounce and floats it toward the hoop. *0.8 seconds.* At the apex of his shot, the ball meets Pierce's hand as the buzzer goes off. Nets win.

The Brooklyn players began celebrating right away. Kyle collapsed to the floor and lay on his back under the basket. I went to pick him up. As I walked over I could see that he was covering his eyes with his hands. I knelt down beside him and leaned down. "I don't care if you made that shot or if you missed it," I told him, "I'm riding with you no matter what." I just sort of blurted it out. I hadn't planned to say it, but as the words left my mouth I realized how much I meant it. We'd come a long way since our first season together. Now we were in the trenches together and I wanted him to know I had his back. By then I'd seen enough of Kyle to know how hard he worked and how much care he put into his craft. I don't have patience for guys that coast on their talent and don't put in the work (which would describe a bigger majority of the NBA than you'd think). I don't want nothin' to do with that. But Kyle put in the work. Like me, he earned respect leading by example. Matter of fact, as it turned out we had plenty in common.

Kyle was raised in North Philadelphia, a rough environment like Compton, where he learned to navigate the poverty, gangs, and violence just like I had. He was raised by a single mom, Marie, and, like me, he stayed close to home for college and went to Villanova to be near his family. We were both dogged by negative media (Kyle was labeled "uncoachable," I was criticized for not expanding my shooting range past the three-point line). We were both new parents planting roots and raising our families in a foreign country (his first-born, Karter, is the same age as Diar, and they're best friends).

Like me, he is guarded, a product of where he was raised. I think not having a father around growing up only amplified that. It would explain the days of him walking around with a hood up over his head and leaving practice the first chance he got. After what he'd been through, he was hesitant to get too close to people. To get attached. I knew the feeling. But once he's comfortable with you, you see a whole different side of him—playful, goofy, like a big kid. Once he lets you in, he's as loyal as they come. Kyle would give you his last without asking any questions—last dollar, last shirt, last meal, anything. His work ethic and passion for the game gave us our first connection, but our friendship just grew from there. Nowadays we're closer than ever. His mom calls me "son" and my mom calls him the same. Kyle and I still speak every day. When he was in the Finals with the Miami Heat in 2023, he would FaceTime me after games, and Diar would call him on game days to tell him he better play well.

I always said that the two of us were like Ray and Claude, Eddie Murphy and Martin Lawrence's characters in the movie *Life*. Ray was a loudmouth—that was Kyle—and Claude was more reserved and down-to-earth. After not speaking to each other in his first season, by year two the barriers between us were starting to break down. On the court, we were emerging as one of the NBA's best backcourts, and that chemistry was spilling over off the court. After Kyle's shot was blocked in Game 7, everything fell in line. We were riding together from there on out.

○   ○   ○

After our surprise run in 2014, we entered the next season with a clear identity (and less roster turnover than any season since I'd been in the league). And we only got better as a team. We earned home-court advantage again, determined to advance past the first round and beyond. We entered the series against the Washington Wizards, who, like us, were driven by their backcourt (John Wall and Bradley Beal). The Wizards added a familiar face that season: Paul Pierce.

We were heavy favorites in the series—and it wasn't hard to see why. We set another record for most wins in a Raptors season, and Kyle was named to his first All-Star team. I had spent my off-season with USA Basketball teaming up with the likes of Harden, Anthony Davis, and Kyrie Irving (and reuniting with Rudy Gay) as we won a gold medal at the FIBA World Cup in Madrid, Spain. I felt like I could hold my own with the best in the world, and I played like it. The Wizards series was ours to lose.

Four games later, we were swept. It sucked. The feeling just . . . sucked. After earning our stripes the year before in the Brooklyn series and bouncing back like we did the next year, we felt we were prepared for what was to come. We carried so much confidence, knowing that as a unit we were heading in the right direction. It was like as soon as the buzzer sounded in Game 4, all of that went out the window.

I just remember how embarrassed I felt. I wanted to hide, but there were cameras everywhere. And I remember how embarrassed we felt as a team, the way we let the whole organization down. It wasn't long before the trade rumors picked up again. That whole thing. It was like the last two years of winning hadn't even happened. Kiara and I had begun shopping around for a home in Toronto and weren't sure if we should put those plans on ice or not.

I knew things were bad when Masai let Lou Williams walk. Lou-Will was an automatic bucket off the bench. He'd been traded to our team from Atlanta before the season and went on to win the NBA's Sixth Man of the Year award with us. I mean, there wasn't even a thought of bringing him back. When I saw that, I called Kyle: "Damn, what's going on? He was one of our best players . . ." That's when I realized it was back to the drawing board.

The noise around the team was getting louder. Outside voices chiming in. Sportswriters and TV talking heads piling on. Back then, I used to pay so much attention to it all—the criticism, the doubters. I read any article written about us and watched everything they said about me on TV. "He's not good at going left, or running screen-and-rolls," they'd say. "He's not a good passer—or a good enough shooter."

I kept a running tally. How one ESPN writer predicted we'd win thirty-three games the same year we ended up winning nearly fifty. How *Sports Illustrated* ranked me sixty-first among all players in 2015 coming off a season where I was one of twenty-four players named to the All-Star team. It used to make me livid. I'd argue with the screen and get all worked up. "What are you doing that to yourself for?" Kiara would ask me. "Don't read that shit. Just ignore it."

I've since learned how to do that. It becomes toxic when you start playing to please others instead of playing for yourself. But for the longest time I used the noise as fuel. It was my cheat code, the motivation I needed to come back stronger. I can't go left? I spent one summer learning how to write with my left hand to help build strength (after a month or so I was neck-and-neck with Diar in terms of our handwriting). I wanted it to be obvious each season that I had spent my summers getting better and better. Every negative thing they said about me stuck in my head. I wanted to debunk all of it. I developed a mantra: "Prove 'Em." I got it tattooed on my wrist. Prove them wrong. I lived by that, every day.

With the way our season ended, the criticism, and the trade rumors, it felt like we were all on the hot seat. If anything went wrong at any point, the team was going to blow it all up. I felt huge pressure on myself heading into the following year. And you know what they say: Pressure bursts pipes. But it can also make diamonds.

I was beginning to feel like an established veteran. I had a growing reputation in the NBA for my footwork and mid-range game, which allowed me to not only get buckets but also get to the free-throw line whenever I wanted to—at least that's what it felt like at times (in the 2015–16 season, only James Harden hit more free throws than I did). I'd learned the importance of footwork from guys like Kobe, who told me to study soccer players, and Sam Cassell, who had taught me how to combine positioning with the pump fake, which became a go-to weapon for me. It got to the point where all I had to do was lift my chin an inch or two and defenders would be up in the air expecting me to shoot.

Indiana's coaches saw it coming. Their players didn't. So during our first-round series in the 2016 playoffs, Indiana implemented a rule that if one of the Pacers bit on my pump fake, he'd be fined. Other teams had the same type of rule. I heard that Cleveland, for example, fined their players for falling for the shot-fake, too. I took it as a sign of respect. As a hooper, I embrace the challenge of having to figure out a counter to their counter. The Indiana series was another close call. Just like the previous year, we entered our first-round matchup as heavy favorites after setting a new Raptors franchise win record for the third year in a row. Kyle and I were playing out of our minds and both made the All-Star game, which took place in Toronto. That whole season felt like we'd emerged as a basketball town after years of being overlooked. We were on the NBA map.

Indiana ended up pushing us to seven games. In the do-or-die game, I led the way with 30 points and our team was off to the second round for the first time in fifteen years. Against Miami in the second-round I drew a matchup with Dwyane Wade, probably the toughest dude to guard of them all. Again, the series went to seven games. Kyle went *off* in the series. In the first game, trailing by three with seconds on the clock, he nailed a half-court shot at the buzzer to send the game to overtime, and dropped 35 points in the deciding Game 7. We made it hard on ourselves, but getting through back-to-back seven-game series made us stronger. We emerged with a new sense of confidence. Each guy did his part to complement one another. Nobody was playing for money, for contracts. We were playing for one another—which can be surprisingly rare in the NBA—and it showed. No Raptors team had ever made it to the East Finals. I wore that shit like a badge of honor.

As soon as the ball tipped off in the conference finals against the Cleveland Cavaliers and LeBron James, you could just feel the intensity dialed up compared to the first two rounds. There are only four teams left in the playoffs and the whole world is watching. It was such a new experience for most of us. Plus, across the court is one of the greatest players to ever play the game. Playing against 'Bron seemed impossible. He had just come off four straight Finals appearances with the Miami Heat and two titles before returning to Cleveland the year before. It wasn't just his skills—there wasn't a single hole in his game by then—or his physicality—he was a football player on the court and could exert his will on your team like nobody I've ever played before or since. LeBron is such a student of the game and a savant on the court, he doesn't just know his playbook—he knows yours, too. Every action, every counter.

Well, from the jump it was a learning experience. Game 1, we got beat, 115–84. Game 2, we got beat, 108–89. Afterward, you couldn't turn on a sports channel without hearing "They're done," whenever they were talking about us. On the trip home from Cleveland after Game 2, I told the guys, "Let's just win at home, take home court, and anything can happen from there." We did just that. We won our next two games at home to tie the series 2–2. But we didn't have enough to get over that hump. The next two games in Cleveland were blowouts. We just ran dry. They had the more experienced team, and we just didn't know how to close it out.

We flew back from Cleveland that night. There were fans waiting to greet us at the airport. Thousands had gathered in Jurassic Park to watch the game outdoors on a big screen. There were still fans there when I arrived back home, long after the game ended. They were chanting "We the North!" like we had just won it all. It was so cool to see fans in the city—and across the whole country—embrace basketball like never before. Watching that scene, I couldn't help but think of what the fans were like when I first arrived. They were always supportive, but in the early days it seemed like hoops was an afterthought. The team used to have a promotion that if we scored 100 points—win or lose—fans would get a voucher for a free slice at a local pizza chain the next day. I can't tell you how many fourth quarters I played in where the fans were just chanting "Pizza! Pizza! Pizza!" down the stretch. Now? They were electric and quickly established a reputation as some of the league's most passionate fans.

Later that year, I passed Chris Bosh to become the Raptors' all-time leading scorer. People thought I was crazy when I tweeted "I got us," after Chris left the team following my rookie year. But here we were, etching our name in record books, competing for a title, and putting Toronto basketball on the map. It was like the franchise, the city, and I had all grown up together.

That off-season in 2016, on the very first day of free agency, I signed a five-year extension to stay in Toronto. I was very aware of what the Raptors fans had gone through in the past when it came to star players. The whole story of the franchise was that stars come and then they want to leave. From Damon Stoudamire, to Tracy McGrady, Vince Carter, Chris Bosh . . . That was the narrative: Nobody wanted to be there. But I grew up idolizing Kobe, who spent his entire career on one team. The stars from the eighties on my VHS tapes who jumped off my screen back in Compton—Magic, Bird, Dr. J, Alex English—they all spent their NBA careers with one team. I wanted the same for myself. I wanted to establish my own legacy, and I had a whole vision of my career in Toronto. In my mind, I wanted to shatter every single record in Toronto history. I wanted my name to be intertwined with Raptors basketball forever. In all honesty, I never even gave a thought to signing anywhere else. I wanted to go through the good and the bad. The winning, the losing. I was going to stick it through no matter what.

Because, to me, to be able to experience the whole spectrum with one organization was a measure of success. I worked my ass off to be in a position where I could grow with that place. Toronto had become home. I was raising my family in Toronto. Kiara was pregnant with our second daughter, Mari, by then and we bought a home in Etobicoke, a suburb west of downtown, to make room. There was never a real discussion about leaving. Kiara and I never sat down at the dining-room table and weighed our options. None of that. I was Toronto for life.

Everything seemed to be moving at a very fast pace, and I didn't exactly have time to relax that summer—I was headed to Rio de Janeiro as part of Team USA to compete for gold at the Olympic Games. When I first came to the NBA I wanted to experience everything the league had to offer, and that included the opportunity to be an Olympian. I'd watched the '92 Dream Team and the 2000 Team USA squad on tape so often as a kid. And after working with Kobe as he prepared to represent the red, white, and blue in Beijing, I was glued to the TV during each USA game in 2008, hoping to one day be a part of the experience.

We brought back much of the same group that had won the FIBA World Cup two years before in Spain—Klay Thompson, Kyrie Irving, DeMarcus Cousins. But the team wanted to add some veterans to the mix, to get some adults in the room. In my mind there was an obvious name: Kyle Lowry. Turns out the minds that run USA Basketball agreed, and that's how Kyle came to join the roster. I didn't have to advocate for him or nothing. He made the Olympic squad off his own success. Being the dog that he is, Kyle fit the team perfectly.

I was on the fence about playing altogether. Kiara's due date was at the end of August, right near the closing ceremony. Between training in Las Vegas and the trip to Brazil, joining the Olympic squad meant that I would be gone most of the summer. I didn't want Kiara to go through the end of her pregnancy alone, and it broke my heart every time I had to leave Diar to go to work. But Kiara said it was a once-in-a-lifetime opportunity and encouraged me to suit up.

The Olympic experience wasn't quite what I had envisioned. We didn't stay in the athletes' village with the rest of the Olympians. I guess they thought we would stick out too much or be a distraction. Or maybe they figured a group of wealthy tall dudes like us wouldn't want to spend a couple weeks living in a dorm-like setting, which would have been fine by me. Instead, they set us up on a yacht anchored offshore. I had some good friends on the team besides Kyle, like Paul George and DeAndre Jordan, so it was cool hanging out, but the routine became so repetitive it felt like the movie *Groundhog Day*. And living on that boat quickly became a grind. So by the time we had a game to play, we were all so hyped just to be doing something different. We cruised to gold.

Two days after the gold-medal game, Mari was born. Right out of the gate she was the total opposite of Diar and me. For the most part, Diar is laid-back, quiet, stays to herself. Mari is more like her mom. She's the energetic one. She's active, loud, and goes nonstop. As Mari got older, she loved dressing flashy and being on center stage, the life of the party. My girls are such a blessing. They ground me in ways they'll probably never know. At the end of the season I'm excited for the time I know we'll get to spend together. They help me get off the roller-coaster of the previous season and just chill. Besides, my kids weren't going to ask—or probably care—about what Daddy does when he's at work. Sometimes that's all I could ever want.

CHAPTER 10

In November, at the beginning of the 2017–18 season, Kiara and I separated. It's hard to pinpoint exactly what happened— it wasn't one incident, but more of an accumulation of things. We had started together so young and everything was moving so fast for both of us that it was like we never had a chance to catch up. We had gone from being a couple of kids dating in college to having a couple of kids of our own while navigating the demands and attention that come with being a star athlete in a billion-dollar industry. It was taking a toll. We were too emotionally exhausted to give our relationship the attention it deserved. Things would flare up, like with any couple, but we never put the time in to tend to the matter at hand. We just kept sweeping things under the rug. I thought I'd gotten pretty good at that, but we reached a breaking point. The feeling was mutual. I never looked at it like it was "The End." We had a friendship that stemmed from deeper than anybody could understand and we had been through so much together. We created humans. We built a family together in another country. We were always going to have a connection and foundation of love and respect, and were going to raise our girls together. But we needed a break. Life, man. Nobody said it was supposed to be easy.

Kiara and the kids went back to L.A., where we had just bought a home. I stayed in Toronto by myself. The first night alone I missed my girls so much, I couldn't sleep and stayed awake all night until the sun came up. Still, I didn't have time to process what was happening. We were in the middle of our season, and I had to lock in. But I just wanted to escape. I felt flooded with anger and pain. So I did what I'd always done. I hid myself in the work.

But not even work could stop life from happening. It was a frigid, snowy late-December night in Toronto. We were playing the Philadelphia 76ers, an Atlantic Division rival, in our last game before the Christmas holiday. We wrapped up the game, a comfortable win to send us into the holidays in a good mood. But after I went back to the locker room and had a shower, I was getting dressed when I got a phone call from my mom: Dad was being rushed to the hospital.

As he was getting older, there had been some incidents where we had to get an ambulance before—I remember one time he fell and hurt his hip badly. This time, Mom said, he had been sick all day and she thought it might have been food poisoning. She called him an ambulance out of caution and they were taking him to Cedars-Sinai Marina del Rey Hospital. Things hadn't been easy for Mom lately, either. Her lupus was beginning to make even everyday tasks, like picking up the phone, difficult. I told her I was heading home that night anyway, and would head to the hospital as soon as I landed.

On the flight home, something didn't feel right.

By the time I got to Cedars-Sinai it was past midnight in L.A. I walked through a maze of hallways and was reminded of visiting

Dad fifteen years earlier when he had his stroke. Sure enough, when I got to his room the doctors told me he had suffered another one. He was passed out when I saw him, exhausted or on sedatives. Even so, I knew Big Dog was a fighter and I figured he'd be out in a week. Tops two. He ended up in and out of there for the next two and a half years.

I began flying back and forth as much as I could. I told Masai and the team about my situation, and they were supportive. I didn't want to be a distraction, so I'd find any time in the calendar when we had more than a day between games, and charter a plane from Toronto (or wherever we were playing that night) home to L.A. to be with Dad. Every time I saw him, he was changing for the worse. I had never seen him so physically weak. My dad was always at my games any chance he got. You couldn't miss him—he'd be the guy wearing a jersey with my number and "DeRozan Dad" stitched across the back, yelling at my ass to get back on defense. Now he was in no condition to travel. I remember he showed up to one game in L.A., but just leaving his bed had left him exhausted.

Kyle's locker was right next to mine at this point. My teammates knew why I was coming and going all the time, but I only shared the details of my dad's stroke with Kyle. And he was the only person on the team who I talked to about the situation with Kiara and the girls. I felt I could trust Kyle with anything. We shared a love for our craft and knew firsthand how basketball offered an escape. As a kid, Kyle rarely saw his father even though he lived around the corner. Raised by a single mother with no means in a dangerous environment, he needed that escape. The court became the only place he could feel safe and in control of his destiny. I knew that feeling as well as anybody. And Kyle knew that. When I was going through my worst, he would lean into my locker stall before games, when the rest of our teammates were talking among themselves, and look me in the eyes. "All right, D," he'd say, "let's go to our happy place." It would lift me up and give me the motivation to keep pushing through. When games were over, he'd put an arm around me on our way back to the locker room and say, "Now back to reality. You got this."

On New Year's Eve, Dad was in the hospital, Kiara was home in L.A. with our girls, most of my teammates were out partying, and I was in the gym, alone. New Year's was never a big deal to me. I never went out partying and going crazy at midnight and all that. After Davian, it just didn't feel like a time I wanted to be celebrating. So I just treated it like any other day, went to the gym and fell into my routine. There's a ritual I've been keeping for as long as I can remember, the same steps and progressions. I start casual, getting my body warm, and then work my way to a sweat at full game speed. I've picked seven spots on the floor, and I go from one to the next. At each spot I have to make ten shots of different types. A straight jump shot, shooting after a pump fake, off-the-dribble shots, side-step shots. No imaginary defenders or nothing. Just me and the hoop. I don't leave until I've made 450 shots. Eventually, you fall into a rhythm and your mind lets go and your natural instincts take over. That way, once you're in a game situation, fatigued as hell and managing a million different things, everything becomes second nature. You can make a move and then, depending how the defense reacts, engage a counter-move in microseconds without even thinking about it. That's why you put in the work.

The next afternoon, January 1, 2018, we played the Milwaukee Bucks.

"Let's go into our zone," Kyle said before the game, and I was on my shit from the opening jump. I just kept attacking. I thought about Dad, Kiara. Attack. Attack. Attack. I thought about the fights I got into at school. Attack. Attack. Attack. I thought about how everyone on the court across from me was probably out partying into the wee hours the night before. I sliced and diced my way through the Bucks defense, feeling like I could get to the basket whenever I wanted. Everything was falling. I hit a pair of three-pointers in the first quarter, scored acrobatic layups with Milwaukee's players all over me, and went to work in the mid-range with a flurry of moves the Bucks had no answers to. *I was working last night. Where were you?!* I thought as each shot dropped through the net. It was gratifying. I ended up with 52 points—a career high. On the way off the court, as we entered the tunnel toward the locker room, Kyle pulled me aside.

"Back to reality," he said. "You got this, D."

CHAPTER 11

That year, 2018, the NBA All-Star game was held in Los Angeles. It was lining up to be a big homecoming for me. Our team was in the midst of our best season yet, and despite everything I was going through off the court—or maybe because of it—I was having the best year of my career and was named to the All-Star starting lineup. I'd made three All-Star teams before, but to take that stage in front of my home crowd was the kind of thing I dreamed about growing up.

Between flying back and forth to visit Dad in the hospital, and everything going on with Kiara and me, there was nothing I wanted more than a break. It had been more than a month since I'd seen my girls, and all I wanted to do was spend time with my daughters, Diar and Mari, to take advantage of the rare weekend at home. I wanted to give them the time they deserved, which seemed impossible to find from September to May each year. But deep down I knew how hard that would be.

As February 18 approached, my cell phone was going off like never before. It seemed like everybody I knew from back home was hitting me up, including old friends back in Compton I hadn't spoken to in years, wanting me to come to this party or that public appearance, or tickets to the game, or to come and hang in the hood.

Earlier in my career, when I was younger, I would have been all into it. But now I felt an urge to get away from it all. In just a few short years my life had changed dramatically.

I wasn't even home in California yet, but text after text, voicemail after voicemail kept blowing up my phone. Yet another face from my past reappearing after years, clout-chasing without a hint of shame. I left most of them unread and unanswered. Fact is, there just aren't many people who are still in the hood living that gang life, old high school friends, who I can still deal with on an everyday basis. I just can't take the bullshit. My whole thing is: You have to want better for yourself. Whether you're a pro athlete chasing your next contract, or a dude from the ghetto without a pot to piss in, I need to see you put in an effort to improve your situation. And so many people from back home just didn't. It was like they were permanently in quicksand. There's no solution-based approach to any problems in that world, other than somebody going to jail or dying. If that's all you know and you're stuck in that mindset, it can put you in such a dark place.

I wanted to retain a connection to my roots, and I was proud of the man that Compton helped turn me into, but the reality was, I was living in another world now. It's why I made an effort to come back and spend time with kids in the community, opening my gym and holding free camps each summer. I wanted them to see someone like me, who made it out and made something of myself, and know that they can, too. I've always said I owe who I am to where I grew up, the good and the bad. But I couldn't live in that world anymore. I had a family. I had responsibilities. I was a provider and a protector.

For years, since I'd been in the NBA, I'd get phone calls from old friends. "Hey, Deebo! Did you hear, man? So-and-so just got killed! They're saying his baby-mama was messing with this other dude from the next hood, and he confronted the dude and took a bullet in the chest." Eventually it hit me: Everything in that story you just told me was fucking negative. Every single part of it. *How are you still doing this?* I couldn't imagine living the same way today as I was fifteen years ago. I love everybody I came up with, don't get me wrong, but at some point you need to want better for yourself.

I just didn't have the energy for it anymore. I'm hearing about people I knew from back in the day up to their same old shit, and meanwhile I'm at home on the couch, watching cartoons with my little girl and she's telling me about a new planet they just discovered in the galaxy, or whatever else she'd learned in school that day. I was living my life on a completely different spectrum. I wanted to be a part of telling a positive story for once.

I know how hard it can be, especially when you only know how to live one way. There's a phrase—"Hurt people hurt people"—that makes me think of the world around me in Compton, where you responded to aggression with more aggression. To me, the best characterization of "Hurt people hurt people" was the villain the Joker from the *Batman* franchise. I always related to him— a few years back I even got a tattoo of Heath Ledger's version from *The Dark Knight* across my right shoulder. He reminded me of a lot of people I grew up with. Misunderstood. Dealt a terrible hand, not knowing how else to cope but to lash out and keep the cycle of negativity turning.

I can't speak for other NBA athletes, or other public figures, but I know that I've been in a constant battle with this feeling of wanting to remain normal. But in my line of work, people perceive you a certain way, and you can feel like you have to live up to that. The more you fall into that cycle, the more you're caught up in it. Then before you know it, you lose your true self to your perceived self. I've seen it happen to a million guys. But I was determined not to let it happen to me. I've never been above using the public bathroom, and I'm always surprised when people see me browsing the cereal aisle at a Target and ask "What are *you* doing here!?" as if I can't fuckin' shop in the same places as everybody else. The pressure to stay "normal" was eating away at me. Especially being a leader on our team. That meant that every game, win or lose, the focus and attention—the noise—would fall onto me. I understood it was part of the deal. But a part of me desperately wanted to just blend in with the rest of the world. To be able to grab a seat on a park bench and eat a burrito and laugh at some meme on my phone without having people approach me, or cameras being shoved in my face.

○   ○   ○

I kept having this same dream around then: Waves are crashing around me, rising from the sea and falling like office towers being detonated. In the distance I can see dark storm clouds muscling in. The roar of thunder rattling my eardrums as the charcoal sky puts on an electric light show. In an instant the clouds appear above me, raining down hail that crashes down like meteors, forming craters the size of basketballs in the ocean surrounding me. There isn't another soul in sight. I'm in a kayak, alone, in the middle of the sea. I don't remember how I got here. And I have no idea how to get back to safety. It's the feeling of nightmares. The water surrounding me begins spinning as a massive whirlpool begins to form. I can feel it take control of the boat and pull me toward a massive void in the center. Suddenly it's not the raging waters around me I'm worried about, but the endless pit engulfing me. There's always more going on in the depths than at the surface. I grip my paddle tightly, plunge it into the sea, and begin paddling furiously like a boxer working a speed bag. It's no use. The force of the water spins me around like a lone sock in a washing machine. The kayak fills with freezing rainwater and starts to submerge as the saltwater rises up past my neck. Yet for some strange reason, I stay perfectly calm amid the chaos.

This is what I feel like when I'm at my lowest. Helpless. Stuck. On the brink of being swallowed up by an angry sea. You paddle and fight and claw but there's not a damn thing you can do about it. It's like Tom Cruise and Emily Blunt in the movie *Edge of Tomorrow*, gearing up day after day for a battle you know you're going to lose.

I had the dream on the flight to LAX from Chicago, where we had just beat the Bulls, on Valentine's Day on the eve of All-Star weekend. Only the sudden contact of the wheels with the runway jolted me out of it. I could feel the sweat through my T-shirt as I roused myself awake.

It was my fourth All-Star appearance and second as a starter, but my first time playing on the NBA's showcase stage in front of my hometown. Like the kayak in the sea, I was being tugged and pulled and pushed in every direction. It felt like every single person I knew in the city was reaching out, asking when they were going to see me, wanting me to get them into this event or that event. I didn't want to see or talk to anybody. Until the game on Sunday night, I just wanted to lie low.

When I stepped off the airplane, my cousin DeShaun was there waiting to drive me home. As we made our way through the city we passed through downtown L.A., which was lined with billboards promoting All-Star weekend. We drove past the Ritz-Carlton and I rolled down the tinted window. Hanging across the side of the fifty-story building was an enormous banner with my name and face plastered across it. So much for lying low.

° ° °

We were in the basement of my crib, where we always ended up hanging out. Besides the huge TV and a pool table with blue felt, there was also a giant mural paying tribute to Compton painted on the walls down there that featured street maps from the neighborhood and street signs reading "Nord" and "Aranbe," the corner where Grandma lived.

Outside, a Sprinter van that I had rented waited patiently on the driveway, motor running, to drive us to downtown L.A. to a Kendrick Lamar concert (I was supporting one of Compton's own) to kick off the weekend, and then to a party hosted by Kenny "The Jet" Smith that I was scheduled to appear at. I was sprawled out on the gray suede couch. I couldn't find the energy to sit up, or even keep my eyes open. "All right, let's roll," one of my cousins announced. I couldn't move. It felt like my whole body had shut down and my brain was refusing to let me leave. *What's happening to me?* I didn't know if I should ask for a doctor or to force myself up and try to catch a second wind.

I was raised to push through. Whatever it is, you need to push through. That was life in Compton. Nobody ever talked about "mental health" or asked if you were feeling all right. Ain't nobody feeling sad for you, because we're *all* struggling. Every day was a bad day, so what are you going to do—cry about it? Nah. You find something that keeps you moving forward. Basketball. School. Gangs. Whatever gets you through the day. That mentality had gotten me to where I needed to go. It took me out of the hood and into a world of comfort and security. But, looking back, I was just pouring sugar over shit. We all were.

I was naïve to think that just because I had moved on to bigger and better, I was suddenly better myself. Naïve to think that growing up in that cycle of pain, fear, and forging onward hadn't left scars, and that I still didn't carry the weight and consequences every day. In truth, it was crushing me.

Growing up, I would have never dreamed of sharing my emotions, of saying how I truly felt. Sad, mad, disappointed, vulnerable, afraid. You kept it to yourself and buried it somewhere deep inside you. The message was never "Tell me how you're feeling." Instead it was, "Hey, if you get in a fight today, you better not come home crying about it." You just had to keep moving on. That way of life applied to even the most painful moments, like losing Davian. I think about Davian all the time, but I don't really do anything special to mark the anniversary of his death. Where I come from, you almost had to act like it didn't exist, because it would weigh so heavily on you if you held on to it.

I learned to channel my anger and use it as motivation. My anger was a means to run faster, to jump higher, to stay in the gym that extra hour, no matter how sprained your ankle is. Basketball was my coping mechanism for the anguish I'd gone through. It was just like the kids I knew who totally loved going to school, because it meant they were guaranteed at least one meal per day. That's how I looked at sports. If I can push through and just get onto the court, then I can escape my reality. And that's the role the game plays for me to this day.

Suddenly, I couldn't keep pushing through anymore. "D, you comin'? Let's go!" a voice came from upstairs as everybody made their way to the van. My body stayed glued to the couch. I tried to stand up, but my legs wouldn't cooperate. My eyelids felt heavy. I could barely muster up the words: "Nah, go on without me."

○   ○   ○

The house emptied out. With the girls asleep upstairs, the house was finally quiet. But instead of peace and calm, the sounds of my youth filled my mind. A couple of hours passed, and I was finally able to peel myself off the couch and head upstairs to try to get a full night's sleep for the first time in who knows how long. I lay there awake for what seemed like days but was probably more like thirty minutes. Defeated, I grabbed my phone and began aimlessly scrolling on YouTube. Eventually, I came across an interview with Jim Carrey talking about mental health and depression. I'd always had a fascination with Jim Carrey. But not because of his movies or any of the roles he's played.

From as far back as I can remember, I was enamored with the life stories of people who overcame a rough environment or upbringing to make something of themselves. His story was top of my list. The more different someone's upbringing was from mine, the more I wanted to know. It was just like all those hours I'd spent alone at the beach at night, lost in the moon and wondering what else was out there. I knew there was more to the world than Compton—for better *and* worse. As bad as it was where I grew up, I knew other people had their own experiences to conquer. I wanted to know what motivated them.

Carrey was born and raised in Canada, near Toronto. When he was twelve, his dad lost his job and he wound up homeless. For months, his family lived out of a yellow Volkswagen bus on a campsite while everybody—Jim, his parents, and his three siblings—took shifts working as janitors. Carrey dropped out of high school to work a factory job and help support the family. With the dream of changing their fortunes forever, he was driven to escape poverty and rise up the comedy ladder. Sure enough, by twenty-one he was on *The Tonight Show*. Incredible.

My favorite Jim Carrey story: Long before he was a movie star, when he didn't have a pot to piss in, he wrote a check to himself for ten million dollars and dated it ten years into the future. He kept it in his wallet for years. Just before the date was about to pass, he landed a job, *Dumb and Dumber*, that paid him exactly ten million. His dad ended up passing away before the movie came out. At the burial, he put the uncashed check in his dad's pocket.

As I watched Carrey talk about his upbringing, I started thinking of my own childhood. My uncle Kevin dying. My cousin spending my childhood locked up. Davian. Countless other friends and family members gunned down. All of the funerals. The feeling of having to reckon with it all each time I stepped onto the court.

The difference between sadness and depression, Carrey explains in the interview, is that sadness is the result of things that happen to you.

"Depression," on the other hand, he said, "is your body saying 'Fuck you, I don't want to be this character anymore.'"

I turned the volume up and sat upright.

He explained how for him, the word "depressed" is another way of saying "deep rest," and that's what your body and mind is calling out for in your lowest moments. It was a concept he said he'd learned from a British writer and self-help teacher named Jeff Foster.

The more I listened, the more familiar it felt. I started making connections. Like all of these parts of my life that seemed unconnected became intertwined. The sleepless nights. The weight of my childhood and the pressure to succeed. A lifetime of trauma swept under the rug.

I'd never been diagnosed with depression. Shit, I'd never even been to therapy—well, once, years earlier, the Raptors hired a team therapist for us to talk to. I didn't take it seriously at all. I was too young, too proud, too naïve about the whole process. I had one session, in a makeshift office in Air Canada Centre back in Toronto, and bullshitted my way through it all. *Yeah, yeah, childhood was rough, blah blah blah.* I couldn't allow myself to indulge in therapy because, one, I didn't know how, and, two, I wasn't willing to consider that a therapist could actually help me work through my problems. I had built up such an impenetrable wall when I was younger. It was like if I couldn't relate to you then I wasn't going to be comfortable enough to open myself up to you. I always thought about it like if you walk into a movie theater and there are two rows of people—one is full of people you know and the other is made up of complete strangers. Which row are you gonna sit in? I took that immature mindset into that therapy session with me. *You don't know me, you don't know what I've been through. You're just asking questions you were taught to ask so you can get whatever it is you're trying to get out of me.* It was like being back in school, questioning the teacher about where the textbook was getting its information from. *How do you expect me to share my traumas with you?*

But this was different. It felt like I was finally able to put a name to this feeling I was carrying around with me my whole life, and had been amplified in recent months. It was nearly 3 A.M. by now and I had another full calendar the next day—All-Star practice, media availability, scheduled appearances, reunions with family and friends. I was so cooked, I just wanted to escape. I jumped into the shower before going to bed, trying to wash this feeling off of me. It didn't work. I got out, dried off, and headed to sleep, dreading having to do this all over again tomorrow. Usually when I'm feeling something, I just hold it in until the feeling eventually passes. This time—and I can't explain why—I wrote it down for the whole world to see. I grabbed my cell phone, opened Twitter, and typed, *"This depression get the best of me . . ."* and hit send. I turned the phone on silent, closed my eyes, and lay back. I could feel my head sinking into the pillow. *Deep rest,* I thought. *That's what I need.* Slowly, the noises in my head began to fade.

○ ○ ○

When I checked my phone the next morning, I was greeted by floods of missed calls and text messages. *What the hell?* At first I thought maybe somebody had died, but half of the missed calls were from my agent, AG. I'd managed a solid few hours of sleep, but the day was off to an early start because I had to drive across the city to downtown L.A. for Saturday's media day at All-Star weekend. I was tired, but I threw on a hoodie and tucked my phone in the pocket of my sweatpants. I kissed the girls, said my goodbyes, and hit the road.

The phone rang in the car—it was my agent again—and this time I picked it up. I've had the same agent since I left college. He's practically family to me. "Man, that tweet you sent," he sounded like he was on the border between worried and apprehensive, "the NBA is asking if everything is OK with you."

"Huh? The NBA?"

"The league office is worried about you. They want to schedule a well-being check-in. Plus," he said, "I've had reporters calling me nonstop. I'm pretty sure you're going to be asked about this all day."

I thought he was overreacting. The way I saw it, all I had done was shared an honest moment—the kind of thing countless people are feeling on any given day. Neither of us realized it at the time, but it was a perspective that hadn't been expressed by an athlete at my level on that kind of platform.

When I arrived at the Convention Center, I was taken to a ballroom with a long row of tables full of basketballs for me to sign. My shoulders sank. I just wanted to go back to the house and hang with the girls. I picked up a silver Sharpie and began to scrawl my name.

"Hey, D, are you *good*?"

I looked up to see a pair of my all-star teammates, Kyrie Irving and Kevin Love. I was tripped up by the level of concern in their voices. Or maybe it was the way they were looking at me differently. "No, really, is everything OK?"

"Me? Yeah, I'm fine," I said. "What's up with you two?"

I wrote my tweet during a moment of vulnerability and transparency. But that moment had passed. Now I was on the job, so to speak, doing my duty. So I went back to being myself, suppressing my true feelings and sweeping it all under the rug. Deep down, their worry meant a lot to me.

When it came time to face the media, things went smooth. As I settled into my seat on a podium, surrounded by microphones, a meaty hand gave me a big pat on the back. I looked up over my shoulder: It was Kyle. I felt a bit more at ease. For over a half-hour I fielded questions. About the Raptors' playoff struggles and why this season would be different. About my homecoming weekend in L.A. There weren't many questions about my tweet. It was almost as if nobody knew what or how to ask me about it.

A few days later I did an interview with Doug Smith, the longtime Raptors reporter for the *Toronto Star*. I opened up in some more detail about my challenges with mental health, about the difficulties of overcoming my upbringing and the scars you carry with you when you grow up in that world. "It's one of them things that no matter how indestructible we look, we're all human at the end of the day," I said. "It's nothing I'm ashamed of."

I would never have felt comfortable enough to begin to share my story when I was a younger person. This was a new thing for me. It's not a conversation I ever had with my parents or friends, because where I grew up you protected your feelings and, no matter what, never showed any sign of weakness. Just like Dad playing dominoes like everything is normal while he can't feel his limbs.

I was worried that, by talking about depression and this feeling of heaviness and exhaustion I'd carried since I was young, I would hurt Mom and Dad. I didn't want them to feel as if they weren't there for me, or hadn't done enough. I spoke to each of them after my media session wrapped. I wanted them to know that nothing was further from the truth. I owed everything to them. My parents were present and active in my life, they showed me love, they showed me direction—so much more than a lot of people I knew could say about their situation. When I opened up to them, Mom and Dad were there for me. They told me they understood and were proud of me, too, and that they knew something had been boiling beneath the surface. They'd seen it at all stages in my life, even if none of us could identify it at the time. Ultimately, it only brought us closer.

My tweet was sparking conversations. On Sunday, the morning of the All-Star game, the head of the players' union, Michele Roberts, was asked about mental health during an interview. "We've been naïve—I'm being kind when I say naïve—in thinking that we didn't have to address . . . our players' mental wellness," she said, adding, "It's a shame that this hasn't been given attention a long, long time ago." Without knowing it, I was bringing the topic of mental-health awareness into the light. But life in the NBA can be so fast-paced. By the time the All-Star game wrapped the following day, it was like someone snapped a finger and it was back to the grind.

o   o   o

Just after the All-Star weekend, we had a two-day break between games and I flew from Toronto home to Los Angeles to visit Dad at the hospital. I stopped into the Barnes and Nobles near my crib to grab something for him to read, and an older, white-haired white man approached me slowly.

"I'm not really into sports," he said, "but I read your story and it helped me so much." He thanked me and walked away. *Huh*, I thought, *that was kinda different*. But before long, all sorts of people were coming up with similar stories and appreciation for me showing that it's OK to not be OK. It has been humbling, to say the least, that what began as a selfish tweet could wind up helping others. It's beyond anything I'd ever imagined.

CHAPTER 12

The conversation surrounding athletes and mental health was gaining steam since my tweet on All-Star weekend. It was crazy to think about the number of athletes who had come forward since to talk about their own journeys and struggles. I thought about Kevin Love, one of the first people I saw after I sent the tweet, and how genuinely concerned he had seemed. A few weeks afterward, he found the courage to open up and share his experience with panic attacks and bouts of depression and embraced being an advocate of mental-health awareness. "To see DeMar step up and say he battles with something every day with his depression, and how it gets to him, that opened the door for me," he said in an interview with ESPN. "With all that he goes through, being from where he's from, being a Black man in America, I can do this too and pay it forward for the next person that needs it. He helped save my life in a way."

I was so honored to have played a role in making him feel as though he no longer had to hide from his reality. I wasn't the first athlete to talk about battles with mental health—a few years earlier, the swimmer Michael Phelps was in the headlines talking about his vulnerabilities—but it was like I helped re-ignite the dialogue. Soon, many athletes did the same. When Simone Biles, the decorated Olympian gymnast, withdrew from the Games due to stress, or when tennis champ Naomi Osaka said she stepped back from competition so she could focus on her mental health, my name would come up. Athletes would reference me while talking about their own battles, and it was beyond humbling. Like an avalanche, those conversations spread throughout society. Growing up, to say that you were struggling was a sign of weakness. Today, you hear people discuss the topic of their mental health as freely as the weather. For my whole life, all my dreams and aspirations were tied to basketball. Success or failure was measured in wins and losses. But this was bigger than sports. To build a career like mine and then have a legacy that transcends the court? Never in my wildest dreams.

○　○　○

For the first time in Raptors history, we finished the season in first place in the East. Expectations were through the roof heading into the 2018 playoffs. In the second round, we found ourselves again facing 'Bron and the Cavaliers. After three games, the series was a disaster. We were down 3–0 in the best-of-seven series and on the verge of getting eliminated by the same team for the third year in a row. 'Bron continued to be our kryptonite. We just didn't have a solution for him. In Game Two he cooked us down the stretch in Toronto. It didn't matter who was covering him—me, OG Anunoby, Serge Ibaka—he kept hitting fadeaway after fadeaway and finished with 43 points. In Game Three in Cleveland, he won the game at the buzzer with a ridiculous one-handed running fadeaway jumper in the corner. In Game Four, he was on the bench with thirty seconds left in the third quarter and his team nursing a 25-point lead. I was bringing the ball up the court, drifting past a screen and waiting for the double-team to come. Swarmed, I crossed the ball between my legs and over to my left hand, while my teammate Fred VanVleet curled to the top of the key.

I hit Freddie with a bounce pass. He raised the ball over his head, and lost it to Cavs guard Jordan Clarkson, who pushed the ball ahead and chased it past half-court on his way for an open layup. I went steaming after him. I thought I timed my jump well enough to get a piece of the ball just as he was going to bring his arms up toward the rim, but when we met in the air my forearm caught the side of his head instead and he went crashing to the floor.

It was an honest foul, but the referees handed me a "Flagrant" penalty—an automatic ejection. I was forced off the court and back to the locker room, frozen in a mix of shock and rage. I sat in a chair, slumped over in disbelief. Not being out there, being able to give myself an opportunity, to put in all this work just to be a spectator when it matters the most. I was furious. Normally I could take my anger out on the court. There was a TV in the locker room. I turned it off. It wasn't supposed to go down like this. We weren't supposed to get swept. I wasn't supposed to be in the fucking locker room down the stretch of an elimination game. This wasn't how I envisioned our season ending.

When the rest of the guys came back into the locker room, it felt like a funeral. The room was quiet—like, hear-the-hum-of-the-lights quiet. To this day I've never been in a locker room with that kind of silence. It stayed like that on the flight home. I think we were all struggling to process what just happened.

I braced for what was coming. All the noise about us as a team and me as a leader. Not to mention the whole "LeBronto" thing.

During the series, the media and fans outside Toronto had already started using the term, saying he owned the city. It gets frustrating, hearing that over and over. Just as frustrating as it was to get knocked out by the same person and the same team year after year. As a competitor, you want to knock off one of the greats and be a part of history. But it never worked out that way. As a team we never had any doubt that we could compete against him. Each year we felt like we were one or two pieces or adjustments away from getting over the hump, and each season felt like a necessary step on the way to my ultimate goal of bringing a championship to the Raptors. We felt so close. To feel like you can reach out and touch something you've only dreamed about, and bust your ass just to fall short each time, that was the most frustrating part of it all. Four days after we were eliminated, the team fired Coach Casey. He had just been named the NBA's Coach of the Year.

○   ○   ○

That summer I started receiving more and more media requests. I was asked to make appearances at events or talks where mental health was the topic. If it felt right, I agreed. Others, I turned down. Being in the public eye for more than a decade, you develop a radar for people who are trying to take advantage of you and are just chasing clout. I wasn't interested in making money or gaining attention by sharing what I'd been through. If I had a chance to help somebody, that's all I needed. One request came in to take part in a series called *The Me You Can't See*, which was co-produced by Oprah Winfrey and Prince Harry. It gave me an opportunity to share my story beyond your typical sports audience, and featured testimonials from people from all walks of life—not just athletes or other celebrities. I thought that was important. People look at athletes, especially NBA players, as larger than life, almost superhero-like, immune to the problems of everyday people. And it couldn't be further from the truth. My story isn't about being a basketball player, it's about being a human being.

The opportunities to talk to kids and people from vulnerable communities in person were the most special. During the off-season in 2018, I was asked to give a talk in Portland, Oregon, to a youth basketball team from the Flathead Indian Reservation in Montana. My message to them was simple: We all struggle, myself included. But you can't keep the pain buried inside forever.

As the kids began to talk about the hardships of their own community, which was plagued by teen suicides, I was reminded of how seriously I needed to take my new responsibility.

There were so many people—in and out of my community—who felt the need to keep everything hidden inside. To show no weakness. I know, because for damn near thirty years of my life, I was one of them. Whether it's a private talk or in public interviews, I was grateful for the possibility that, by talking about my own struggles, I might inspire somebody else to take steps toward connecting with theirs. Speaking with younger people in particular—kids and teenagers who were struggling but didn't know how to show it, or process their pain—gave me a bona fide purpose. I quickly realized that using my voice and platform was mutually beneficial: By sharing the message that as Black men, as athletes, as human beings, it's OK to be vulnerable and to show that vulnerability, I was shedding my own insecurities, too.

But I was conflicted about the role I was being asked to play. I kept hearing people refer to me as a "face," and I never had a clear-cut answer for what, exactly, that was supposed to mean—being a "face" of mental-health awareness. What comes with being an advocate? Can I not make any more mistakes? Can I not still continue to feel? It seemed like such a bold obligation, and I was still only taking the first steps in my own mental-health journey. All I knew was that I didn't have the answers. The best way I could help was by being an example. I couldn't tell you what the "cure" was for trauma, or if one even exists. But I was there to say that I've been through it. And I'm still going through it.

CHAPTER 13

I walked through the large oak doors, past the white marble walls, and into a private dining room at the SW Steakhouse at the Wynn Hotel in Las Vegas. It was mid-July, and Masai, Kyle, I, and the rest of the team had gathered in the dry heat of Vegas in front of the backdrop of the NBA Summer League, an annual showcase for the league's rookies and up-and-coming players, as well as an opportunity for free agents to catch the eye of NBA scouts in the hopes of landing an invite to a September training camp. I always tried to make an appearance at Summer League and put some face time in with our team, joining them in the gym or offering words of encouragement and any advice I can on how to make it in the league. (The year before, the Raptors Vegas squad had featured the next wave of stars like Fred VanVleet, Pascal Siakam, and Jakob Poeltl. This year, the team was headlined by OG Anunoby.) It's a dope atmosphere—there are games being played on two courts from morning 'til night, a hoophead's dream, and for us players, many seeing one another for the first time after battling it out during the season, the

Thomas & Mack Center almost feels like you're attending a family barbecue.

At the Wynn there was definitely a feeling of family among us. We'd been through so much together over the past few years, rising in the ranks and growing both as teammates and individuals. After the way our season had ended, it was important that we escape the darkness and regroup as a team in the light of day, so to speak. Despite the playoff disappointment, there were still positives to take from the season. I had put my name in the Raptors' record books, becoming the team's all-time leader in wins, total games, and minutes played—which seemed crazy given how recently draft night and those earliest days with the team still felt. More important, we'd added to our win total, setting another franchise record and finishing in first place in the East for the first time ever. Although my scoring numbers dropped, I felt I was better than ever and had expanded my game as a playmaker and somebody who can help the players around me. The writers and broadcasters who cover the league and vote for the All-NBA selections at the end of each season must've agreed. For the first time in my career, I was named to the All-NBA team.

There was a buzz in the room as we relived the past year and talked about the season ahead of us. I was still processing what had happened to us against Cleveland, but there was suddenly more reason to believe we could finally make it over the hump the next year. A week or so before, news came out that LeBron was signing a contract to join the Los Angeles Lakers. Each season, we felt that he was the only person blocking our path to reaching the Finals. We wanted to be on that stage so badly but could never find a way to beat 'Bron. With him playing in the West now, the conversation around dinner was all about us now having an opportunity to win it all—at the very least, we were sure we were on track to break through to the Finals.

We knew there was no sugar-coating the way our season had ended, getting swept and embarrassed like that in front of the world. It ate away at me and certainly wasn't doing anything to help my already-sleepless nights. Coach Casey was quickly replaced by his assistant coach, Nick Nurse, a sharp hoops tactician. Case's old-school, success-is-earned-through-hard-work approach had helped ignite our team and turn the franchise around. We went from second-class citizens in the NBA to a perennial East contender on his watch. He allowed me to grow as a player and trusted me with the ball in my hands in countless big situations, and I wished nothing but the best for him and his family.

Seeing and hearing the excitement from the players and staff around the table, for the first time since the season ended I felt at peace with where we were at. New coach, new landscape, new situation. I accepted what lay ahead for us as a group and was excited to continue our journey together. There was reason for hope and a chance for a fresh start.

After we ate, Masai presented me with a plaque commemorating my All-NBA selection as my teammates cheered me on. Everybody raised a glass and toasted me. I didn't want the attention and didn't play for individual awards. I'd been an All-Star, an Olympic gold medalist, and now I was All-NBA. But all I wanted was to bring a title to Toronto. "Here's to us getting it done next year," I said, as we clinked our glasses. As we wrapped dinner, Masai and I chatted about a trip to Lagos, Nigeria, two weeks out, where I was going to meet campers and take part in his Giants of Africa program, a basketball showcase and training camp created to help develop skills and create exposure for young prospects across the continent. He also talked about the next season for the Raptors and what he had up his sleeve. With LeBron out of our way, his plan, he said, was simple: "We're going to run it back."

○   ○   ○

Two nights later, I was back in L.A. and off to a premiere at the famous Mann's Chinese Theatre for the movie *The Equalizer 2* starring Denzel Washington, with no indication that my entire world was about to be flipped upside down. Living in Los Angeles and being such an avid moviegoer, I loved having the opportunity to attend events like this. I avoid the red carpets and whatnot whenever I can, but it's definitely one of the perks of the job that will never get old.

In the middle of the screening, I felt my phone vibrate inside the pocket of my jeans. I squeezed my hand in, discreetly pulled it out, and saw the name on the call display: Masai Ujiri. *Huh?* I was confused. I didn't expect a call from Masai and we had almost literally just returned from meeting in Vegas. I figured it must have been something to do with our Giants of Africa trip, working out some logistics or something. I sent him a quick text. "I'm just at the movies. I'll call when I get out."

"OK," he wrote back. "Enjoy the movie."

I couldn't concentrate on the big screen in front of me. I got this sickening feeling, like I was in the kayak and the ocean waters were beginning to swirl.

I curled my hand over my phone to hide the glare coming off the screen as I checked Twitter and Instagram, searching for any news about the Raptors. I found nothing.

I turned to AG, my agent, who was sitting beside me.

"Masai just called me," I told him, asking if he might know why.

"Just now?" he said, sounding as surprised as I was.

"Yeah, just now. Do you know what's going on?"

"Nah, nah," he said, "I'm sure everything's fine."

So I didn't think nothing of it. I double-checked that my phone was on silent and slid it back into my pocket.

It was just after eleven on the West Coast when the movie ended. On my way out of the theater, I called Masai back. He didn't answer. I made a plan to meet my cousins for a bite to eat at a Brazilian steakhouse called Bossa Nova about twenty minutes away. Soon after the rubber hit the road I was cruising down Pico Boulevard when my phone rang. It was Masai. He didn't waste any time: "Hey, D, uh, I wanted to let you know that we just traded you to San Antonio."

I didn't say anything. Not a word.

"Well, um, the deal just went through," he continued, "and I wanted to let you know first because the news will go public soon. By the morning the whole world will know."

I hung up the phone, pulled over, and just sat there. It might have been five minutes. It might have been five hours. I was too numb to tell. Eventually, I got out of the car and just began walking up and down the street, just wandering, with no destination in mind. I remember that the streetlights and storefront windows seemed blinding. I had been blindsided. I felt betrayed. That was a new one for me. For all the pain I'd gone through in my life growing up, at least I had stability in my immediate family; my parents made sure I grew up in a home where I could trust their word.

The first person I phoned was Kyle. It was three o'clock in the morning back in Philadelphia where Kyle lived. I woke him up with the call and by the sounds of it he must've been in a deep slumber. He was confused, said he couldn't believe it, and told me that no matter what happens next I was going to make it through it all for the better. "Love you, Dog," he said and in a tired, mumbled voice, told me that he would call back as soon as he woke up later in the morning. I hung up and dialed Rudy Gay next, my good friend and old Raptors teammate, who now played for San Antonio where we'd be teaming up once again, this time for the Spurs. He was excited. I was in shock.

I ended our call, headed back to the car, and drove straight to the beach in Santa Monica. I needed to be alone. I left my shoes in the car and found a spot in the sand. I looked up at the moon. It was brighter than I'd ever seen it. *The moon will shine again tomorrow.* Funny, I thought, how it has to be total darkness to really see it like this. When that didn't help, I tried to transport myself back to my childhood, when I'd stare at this same moon and dream of where life would take me beyond Compton. I dreamed of escaping my environment and vowed to put myself in a position where I could bring my family with me. To take care of my parents, Grandma, and her grandchildren like I'd promised. I dreamed of making it to the NBA and continuing to work for the game I loved. I dreamed of experiencing more than what I'd been exposed to growing up and to do whatever it took to jump off the hamster wheel of poverty and violence that I saw so many people around me get caught up in. I had so much to be proud of. But none of it seemed to matter.

I was blindsided by the trade. Completely fucking blindsided. For nine years I gave my heart and soul to Toronto and the Raptors franchise. I gave them all of my love and they gave it back tenfold. They were family. When you spend that long in one organization, going from wide-eyed kid to grown-ass man in front of their eyes, it's impossible not to form connections with the people around you, from the parking-lot attendant to the equipment manager and everyone in between. And then there's my teammates. In the early days, while we were losing and our locker room was full of new faces each year, I got good at detaching from my teammates, of not getting too close. But when you win, it's all different. Winning is like a magnet that draws you together as a group. After years of playoff battles, those were like my brothers. Not to mention the commitment I made to the fans of Toronto. It was all being torn away from me—and I was powerless to do anything about it.

From the beach, I headed to Mom's house, where I had been staying while Kiara was at home with the kids. I didn't tell Mom what had happened. I just gave her a kiss and told her I loved her, that it was late and we should both go to sleep. I turned my phone off and lay down on the couch until the sun came up.

The next morning, it was like All-Star weekend all over again. I turned my phone on to find an endless scroll of missed calls and text messages. *I guess the news is out,* I thought. I turned on the TV and it was everywhere. On ESPN, a ticker ran across the bottom of the screen that read: *Breaking News: Spurs trade Kawhi Leonard & Danny Green to Raptors for DeMar DeRozan, Jakob Poeltl & 2019 Protected 1st Round Pick.* It was surreal. I still couldn't fucking believe it. The phone started ringing. It was Coach Pop, Gregg Popovich, the Hall of Fame head coach of the Spurs, calling me from San Antonio. I didn't pick up. I didn't want to speak to another soul. It was a few days before I could begin to process what had happened, let alone talk to anybody about it. For the next week I barely left my mom's house except to see Diar and Mari.

I was back in Las Vegas the following week for a USA Basketball event. *Everybody* was still talking about the trade—debating which side won and asking me if I ever saw it coming (I didn't). I was feeling overwhelmed, and it wasn't long before I became so tired of people bringing up the trade everywhere I went. I just wanted to smash the mute button, hit fast-forward, and get on with the next season so I could at least get back at peace playing basketball.

One night on the trip I was eating at a restaurant called Mastro's with a group of Team USA staff and former teammates. They were all chatting, and kept trying to include me in their conversation but I couldn't focus. I was googling "places to disappear to." For real.

◦ ◦ ◦

Usually when my friends and fellow players talk about a getaway, they mention somewhere like Las Vegas, or South Beach in Miami, with the nightlife and clubs and bottle service and that whole thing. More power to them. But I didn't want anything like that. I wanted to go somewhere as different from what I knew as possible. I craved fresh, new, different. Anything to bring me out of this funk and help me appreciate the world around me.

So as I was flying in to stay at a ranch in middle-of-nowhere Wyoming and descending toward the airfield, I couldn't help but notice the vast nothingness of it all down there. *This is perfect,* I thought. No blocks of housing developments, or clusters of blinking buildings, or a labyrinth of freeways all stacked on top of one another. Just patches of flatland, farms, and forests. And an immediate sense of calm.

By the time I arrived at the ranch it was nightfall. I stepped out of the coach bus and looked straight up into the night sky. Every star was visible, gleaming, like some sort of welcoming party. I pulled my cell phone out of my pocket and powered it down. The screen turned black and the moon reflected off it as it hung overhead. I looked up and thought about what Dad said.

"The moon will shine again tomorrow."

Through pain comes hope. Hope that tomorrow is a new day where the moon is waiting, reminding us to be thankful that we are here to see it. I settled into my cabin—I wouldn't exactly call it rustic; let's just say it was nothing like Dad's family home in

Louisiana—and powered down for the night. As I lay in bed, I tuned in to the sounds around me. Leaves and branches softly brushing against each other in the breeze. Crickets chirping in the tall grass. The *buzz* of the occasional fly. I closed my eyes and thought about the sounds I heard when I was a kid. The sirens. Gunfire. Helicopters. Commotion. I opened my eyes and listened closely. In the distance a frog croaked. Otherwise it was just . . . quiet. I used to chase this feeling as a teenager, sitting back and taking in the sounds of the waves hitting the shore alone at the beach at night, staring up at the moon so long that I could make out the craters. The peace and quiet—words I knew growing up, but rarely lived.

In the morning, I pulled back the curtains, revealing a real-life painting in front of my eyes. There was a mountain range to the left, overlooking an enormous but still lake surrounded by trees as tall as apartment buildings. With the exception of our childhood trips to Vidalia, I had never been to the true wilderness like this. I was instantly humbled by it all. For the next week, I stayed on the site, except for excursions to hike into the woods to spot bighorn sheep or to fish on the lake, where apart from the call of a bird passing by every now and then, the splash of the lure hitting the water is the only sound you can hear for hours.

Mom had brought up the idea of therapy now and again since I began talking about depression at All-Star weekend. To my surprise, she told me that she had seen a psychiatrist a time or two recently, in the wake of Dad's worsening health. "Sometimes it can help just to talk to somebody," she said, trying in her own subtle way to motivate me to take that same step and pursue therapy of my own. I told her I was happy that she found it helpful, and that I wasn't quite ready myself. I was skeptical of therapy and leery of psychiatrist types. I stayed that way for quite some time.

That's not to say I wasn't healing.

That environment—the great outdoors—became my favorite type of place to visit. The next year, I found myself in Greenough, Montana, a small town of less than two thousand people about twenty-five miles east of Missoula and one hundred miles south of the Flathead Indian Reservation, where the kids from the hoops team I spoke to in Portland came from.

It was nature therapy. And I was hooked.

But like anybody who goes to therapy says, it takes time to make progress. As mind-numbingly beautiful as my surroundings were, and as much as I fucking loved the anonymity of being in the middle of nowhere and the rare chance to exist away from the spotlight, the aches from the trade still followed me. The basketball part, I knew, would sort itself out. I'd put so many damn hours into my craft, and continued to approach the game like a puzzle I had to continually solve, that I had the utmost confidence that I'd put myself in a position to succeed when it came to whatever might transpire on the court.

But I struggled to cope with what, exactly, my family and I were about to go through during what was going to be a major period of transition for all of us. More than once I thought, *How are we going to do this?*

We had bought a home in Toronto that we were going to have to sell while we relocated full-time back to Los Angeles. Diar, who was six, was going to have to say goodbye to all of her Toronto friends—who knows if she would even see them again?—and I couldn't stand the thought of carrying the guilt from that. I was stressed and anxious. But I also didn't want to dwell on those things once I got home. I needed to be the protector for my girls. I wanted to return home and step into action, taking it all in stride to show my children that everything was going to be OK. But inside I was panicking.

On my last night in Wyoming, I called my dad in Los Angeles

to check in. From his hospital bed at Cedars-Sinai, he answered the phone. "DeMar, I'm so happy you called," he said. His voice was raspy and he spoke slowly. Even at his weakest, he was tough as they come. Given everything that happened at All-Star weekend, I was becoming more confident about feeling vulnerable by then. I told him I was worried. Disappointed. Like always, he told me not to worry and reassured me that everything was going to be all right. Once he said that, I stopped holding so much worry about what would happen next.

Deep down, I knew that the move and all of that would sort itself out. So would my time in San Antonio. What I *didn't* know was how, or if, I was going to let go of this pain I was feeling.

I arrived back home the following day, ready to take on the next chapter.

PART THREE

CHAPTER 14

Gutted as I was to be traded from the team I wanted to spend my career with—and just when it felt like we were finally going to get over our demons, no less—I also recognized the opportunity in front of me: I was going to get to play for one of the greatest coaches in history. I knew Gregg Popovich from the USA Basketball program (he was brought in to coach the team after the 2016 Rio Olympic Games that I'd competed in) and obviously from years of competing against him. Coach Pop, as everybody calls him, had overseen one of the NBA's winningest dynasties, capturing five championships between 1999 and 2014. When I arrived, the Spurs hadn't missed the playoffs in nineteen years.

Any concerns I still had about the trade washed away the first time I saw him in person ahead of training camp. "DeMar, I want you to know that I didn't trade you," Pop told me, looking deeply into my eyes with the utmost sincerity. "I traded *for* you." I hadn't realized how much I needed to hear that. It had the same impact on me as when my dad assured me that everything would work out. It was like a switch flipped inside me. *Let's get started.* I didn't choose to leave Toronto, but the more I thought about it, the more I appreciated where I'd ended up. Over two decades of winning basketball, the San Antonio organization had cultivated a reputation and a means of going about their business. Everybody refers to it as "the Spurs way," which basically comes down to committing yourself to your role and the work, being gracious in victory and defeat, and trying to be a good person at your core. I told Pop I wasn't going to have any trouble buying in.

When I talked to Pop about Dad's stroke and the condition it had left him in, and how I had been flying back and forth between Toronto and Los Angeles between games in order to be near him, he was beyond supportive. "Family first" are two words I heard from him often.

I quickly learned that Coach Pop is a real one. We became extremely close, and we spoke constantly—you'd be surprised how rare that can be when it comes to NBA players and coaches. I've known coaches who barely interact with their players outside the huddle. Not Pop. He was always engaging me in conversation—yes, about hoops, but more often than not about life. He'd check in regularly on off-days to see how my kids were doing or how my parents were feeling that day. I felt like he was going out of his way to show that he cared for me as an individual. Turns out that was just Pop being Pop. As much respect as I have for him as a coach (in the history of the NBA, no coach has won more games), I have infinitely more for him as a person. With Pop, what you see is what you get. Given the way my time in Toronto ended, it was refreshing.

From those final days with Toronto—the sweep, the ejection, the "LeBronto" noise—to the trade that sent me from the Raptors to the Spurs, I barely had a moment to stop. It was a whirlwind, and I hadn't even had a chance to process my experience at All-Star weekend. I didn't shy away from talking about my experiences and encouraged others to do the same if I was asked about it or someone came up to me. But I hadn't exactly dealt with my issues. I did what I'd always done and transferred those feelings of anger, frustration, and hurt into basketball. Putting a name—depression—to the heaviness that I carried with me felt like a revelation, and I wanted to learn more and work through it further. I just didn't know how.

Several people suggested I seek therapy as a good next step, but I was on the fence. Inside, I knew that I carried a mountain of trauma from the way I grew up that I never actually confronted. But I was afraid a therapist wouldn't understand the world I came from.

I carried the weight of somebody who had to tiptoe around gangs and other land mines back in Compton. I carried the terror of that little boy not knowing if he or his loved ones would make it through to the next day. But I couldn't imagine opening myself up to a stranger about why. It's always been a major challenge for me to be comfortable around people I didn't know. The more different they are from me, the more insular I become. For the first thirty years of my life that mindset alone made an exercise like therapy—where, by definition, you're opening yourself up to a stranger—impossible.

It wasn't until I was in San Antonio that it changed for me. I was out buying some groceries before practice one day, when an older Black man—older than me, at least—approached me. "I appreciate everything you did," he told me. At first I wasn't sure what he was referring to. "You were willing to talk about the feelings you've been going through," he continued, "and I know that isn't easy." The man began to talk to me about his childhood and the things he had been through. His father was a drug dealer who used to beat his mother, and eventually he and his mom had to leave and start a new life on their own. While I couldn't relate directly to his experience, there was an underlying message of having to face and not hide from the challenges in your life that rang true.

"Oh, I don't think I ever introduced myself," he said. "My name is George. [I'm changing his name.] I'm a therapist." Maybe it was because George was showing his vulnerable side, approaching me like a fellow man and not a clinician. Nothing felt forced about our conversation, or the way he had come at me. Maybe it's because somewhere in my mind I knew I couldn't keep going on like this, harboring my feelings and emotions until my body shut down again. Whatever it was, I agreed to meet up with him again and continue our talk. It never felt like therapy, at least not how I had built it up in my mind—you know, lying on the couch like Tony Soprano, someone sitting over your shoulder taking notes and asking, *"Now how did that make you feel?"* This was different. George would swing by the Spurs' facility after practice and we would just grab a spot to sit and chat, going back and forth sharing stories of growing up, and talking through the pain that often lingers. I told him about Davian and how I blamed myself for not going to get him the day he was shot to death. I told him about my uncle Kevin, and the dozens of funerals I'd attended and the violence that would erupt at them. I told him about my dad pushing me so goddamn hard and yet that somehow it made me love him even more. I told him about Kiara and the girls, and this feeling of constantly chasing after the dream of a calm, peaceful life. He would listen, share his own stories, and talk about what we can take away from our experiences and how we can use them to shape us for the better. "You're living proof that it's possible," he said. I had never really looked at myself in that way before.

We talked about concepts like post-traumatic stress disorder (PTSD), which helped open my eyes to the different ways my past was influencing my present. It had created a defense mechanism that left me always cautious—cautious of what I was going through, and of the people around me. I began to understand that my being guarded with certain people was a survival instinct I had developed.

The whole process felt collaborative and natural. It turns out that was the approach I needed. Our chats throughout my first season in San Antonio broke down the barriers of therapy. It allowed me to embrace just how helpful it can be to talk about your life, to recognize the things we still hold on to as we grow older, and how to process it all through healthy channels.

At the end of the season in April, I was invited to the 2019 Aspen Ideas Festival in Colorado to be part of a speakers' panel event called "Everybody Is Going Through Something." It featured me and Kevin Love, and was moderated by Michael Gervais, a sports psychologist who worked with high-performance athletes, including Pete Carroll's football teams at USC. It was one of my first experiences talking about my mental health in front of an audience like that, and I'm glad I did. I was processing from the stage some of what led me to send the original tweet, and talking about the misconceptions people have about the invincibility of pro athletes. Like we're somehow different and immune to the ups and downs of human experience. "I'm more than a basketball player," I told the audience from my seat onstage. "My kids look at me like I'm the greatest person on earth. They could give a damn if Daddy had a bad game."

Backstage after the event, I was catching up with Michael Gervais. He seemed like an interesting dude from what I'd heard during the panel. He mentioned to me that he was based in L.A. and was going to be there throughout the summer. He suggested we should meet for a few sessions. I told him I'd give it some thought.

Once I settled into my off-season routine back home, I gave Michael a call and told him I was ready to go to work. Michael had also been in Rio in 2016, working closely with the USA volleyball teams, but I never interacted with him then. I wouldn't have been interested, anyway. A lot had changed between then and now. When we started working together, I didn't shy away from our sessions. We discussed the anger and resentment over my upbringing that I carried and how I channeled it into what made me successful. I wanted to understand why, in my dreams, when I feel like my boat is being dragged under the water, I'm strangely calm. He started asking about my dad. I told him how involved Dad had been in my life growing up and how lucky I felt in that regard. About the protective circle he helped form around me to keep me out of the gangs, or simply to keep me alive. We talked about the intense battles on the court we'd shared, and how he used to push me harder than anybody. I told him about stealing his car when I was a teenager and how disappointed he used to get in me when I would act up and get into fights when I was a kid. I told him about how my dad used to lock me in our broom closet as punishment. I remember it was pitch black in there. As a parent today, it seems extreme to me. Back then it was just "tough love." I would scream and cry and kick at the door, asking him to let me out, which he never would. One day, he put me in the closet and I was silent. I didn't kick. I didn't scream. I just stood in the darkness. After a while, Dad opened the closet and let me out. He never put me in there again. I didn't know what to make of all of it, but it was a memory that I'd held on to all these years. "See," Michael said after I told him the story, "that's it. That's why in your dream you're calm while there's chaos around you." He was pinpointing why and how I'd learned to use basketball to cope with whatever else was going on in my life. "A child's biggest fear is being left alone," Michael explained to me. "And after plenty of times of facing that fear—being left in a dark closet, yelling with nobody coming to help—eventually it got to the point where you were able to find calm inside there. You stopped screaming. I think that's where you developed your ability to channel those feelings of hurt and fear into something productive. And that's not easy, DeMar."

Much later, I learned that Michael had also worked closely with Felix Baumgartner, the Austrian skydiver who jumped out of space and landed in New Mexico as part of a stunt for Red Bull back in 2012. Felix was an experienced and confident skydiver who trained for eight months straight just for this one jump. Only problem was, he was terrified of the jumpsuit. Not the jumping. Just the suit. Red Bull had put millions of dollars behind this whole campaign and designed a jumpsuit that was different from what Felix was used to. Each time the guy put it on, he would feel claustrophobic and have a panic attack. He was ready to pull out of the entire stunt. So Red Bull hooked him up with Michael, who worked for months to help him get over his fear of being in this suit, and helped him to realize that he was feeling restricted in other parts of his life, and being inside the tight-fitting suit ignited those feelings. When I heard that, I thought, *Damn, this guy is good.*

There's a lot of comfort to be found when you start to understand more about yourself. It's like you begin to make connections you didn't know were there. Like all of these feelings and events that seemed unrelated can begin to align like branches forming on the same tree. But at the same time, the more I began to unpack my past and the ways it was affecting me today, sometimes it only made me feel more lost. With each "a-ha!" moment came the question: *What else?* If it took me thirty years to tap into my emotions and figure out the source of my pain, or why I need to process my hurt alone, or why I continually find myself in dark places, then what else am I missing? What else am I hiding away from? What else should I be asking in order to unlock more answers about myself? So in a lot of ways, the therapy can become discouraging. But I had to remind myself not to lose perspective. I was in the early stages of discovering myself and satisfied in the progress I was making. My tweet about depression had cracked the door slightly. It would take a lot more work and effort before I could kick it open.

I haven't pursued regular therapy. But it's something I should keep at. If I'm being honest, I tend to fall into the same cycle: I'll take part in therapy sessions for just long enough to feel some progress, and then I back out. Otherwise it's too much to take on all at once. At some point the emotional burden begins to feel too heavy and I need to take a step back, to sit in my thoughts and feelings for a while until I'm ready to indulge in therapy again. I never walk away with all the answers. I never walk away from therapy sessions being "cured." That's not how it works. But therapy has provided me with a better understanding of myself and a passion to continue to help others embark on their own mental-health journeys in any way I possibly can.

○   ○   ○

San Antonio. January 3, 2019. The first game back after New Year's was circled on the calendar: my first matchup against Toronto since the trade. I knew that it was a big game for Raptors fans, but any of the focus on me was offset by Kawhi's return to San Antonio. In San Antonio the fans were making as big of a deal—if not bigger—about Kawhi's first game back. There had been so much drama surrounding the whole Kawhi situation and how it played out with both the franchise and the fans. I never bothered to get caught up in it and heard that there had been an issue with his knee and there were disagreements over his treatment and rehab, and things just soured from there. All I knew was that my Spurs teammates who had been there during all the Kawhi drama *really* wanted to win. I wanted to help them get it done and was happy to not have to feel like the pressure was all on me to exact revenge.

In the locker room before tip-off, we sat and talked about treating it like another game. We were playing great basketball as a team and had won eight out of our last ten. I was taking on a new role as a playmaker and working closely with Pop and his coaching staff. I felt like my game was expanding every night. *Let's just keep it rolling. Don't get caught up in the emotion. Just execute and enjoy.*

As soon as we walked onto the court it was obvious this wasn't just another game. You'd think we were entering the Colosseum for battle, the way the Spurs fans at the AT&T Center were hooting and hollering. It definitely felt strange at first to line up on the other side from Kyle and them guys, but as soon as the ball tipped we were just off to the races. With the crowd behind us, we jumped out of the gate on fire. On one of our first possessions, LaMarcus Aldridge passed me the ball out of a double-team and I shot a high-arcing floater that swished through the mesh. A few plays later, my teammate Derrick White found me cutting toward the hoop on an inbounds play and delivered the ball right into my hands as I erupted to the rim for a dunk. Toward the end of the quarter, Rudy slammed home a dunk to punctuate a 19–2 run. As a team we felt in sync from the jump, and before I knew it, I looked up at the scoreboard and we're up by 20 and it's still the first quarter. I had 20-10-5 at halftime and finished the game with a triple-double—the only triple-double of my career. We crushed 'em. It was just like we were back in scrimmage and I'm tearing them guys up. I felt good for my Spurs teammates, and I'm sure they returned the feeling. And I felt good for the fans, too. The San Antonio crowd was amazing. Not only do they love their team but they really know their hoops.

Still, to me, it's not like Toronto. There ain't nowhere like Toronto.

Nearly two months later, in our first game after the All-Star break, we had a rematch with the Raptors—our second of two games against them during the regular season. This time the game was in Canada. As much as I tried to downplay the emotions of facing off against the franchise I gave my heart and soul to, this one, I knew, couldn't be "just another game."

We arrived on Thursday, the night before the game. It was my first time back in the city since the trade and I couldn't bring myself to go back to our house to pack up and say goodbye. As soon as the wheels of the Spurs' team plane touched down on the tarmac, I felt transported to ten years earlier, the morning after the NBA draft, when I hopped on a plane from New York to Toronto and my life changed forever. We piled out of the airplane and into a bus that snaked its way through Toronto traffic and took us to our hotel.

We pulled up to the Ritz-Carlton hotel on Wellington Street in downtown Toronto. There was a crowd of fans outside the hotel, wearing my number 10 Raptors jersey, chanting my name and showing more love than I could have ever expected. The next morning, when we arrived at the arena for our shootaround, it dawned on me just how connected I had been with this place. I knew everybody there, and they all seemed genuinely happy to see me. It was such a cool feeling. There were arena staffers who I'd seen on their very first day of their job and saw their careers progress over the years. I realized in that moment that we had all shared an experience because, shit, playing for the Raptors was my first job, too. I was on the court, and they were in the concourse, or somewhere else behind the scenes. But we were in it together.

When I stepped out onto the floor for tip-off, the sellout crowd gave me a standing ovation. A little over five minutes into the game, during a timeout, the team showed a video tribute on the Jumbotron with the words "Thank you, DeMar" printed across the top of the screen. Looking at the montage they'd put together was a trip. There was me as a rookie, dunking during games. Holding Diar when she was just a baby. Chopping it up in the locker room with Kyle and the guys. Taking a hug from Drake on the sidelines. My All-Star debut in New Orleans. Our playoff battles together. Fans of all ages and backgrounds posing around the city wearing my jersey. *Damn,* I thought as I craned my neck to look up at the screen, *I really did create so many memories here, didn't I?* After a minute or so the video wrapped and I stood up and waved at the crowd, who were on their feet. It was one of the most touching moments I'd had on a basketball court. But there wasn't time to dwell on it. We still had a game to focus on—and it was shaping up to be a hell of a game. Playing against my old squad brought out a fire in me and it didn't take much to get me hyped to match up against the Raptors. (Around the same time the next year, I threw down my favorite dunk of my career against Toronto: Starting from the top of the arc with the ball in my hands, I surveyed the floor and took a quick screen from my teammate. I faked left, and drove hard to the right, losing the Raptors defender on my tail. I barreled to the free-throw line, took two strides, and lifted off my feet toward the rim, where I was met by the Raptors big man, Chris Boucher. He tried to block my dunk, but it was too late. I slammed that ball through the rim with so much force that

Boucher and I were tangled and fell to the ground together in a heap. It was one of the more physical dunks I'd ever made. Being a guy who was known for a long time as a dunker, I've caught a lot of bodies and put a lot of dudes on posters. Factor in the moment, and that was my favorite one of them all.)

After the tribute video wrapped, the two sides kept battling back and forth all the way down to the wire. The atmosphere in the arena felt like a playoff Game 7. We were down by one with twenty-four seconds remaining, and the Raptors missed a free throw. The ball bounced far off the rim, and I leaped to corral it. I dribbled the ball up toward half-court, Kawhi guarding me closely with Kyle right behind him coming for the double-team. Just before I was about to pass the half-court line, I stumbled and lost the ball. Kawhi picked it up off the ground and took off for an uncontested dunk. That was the ballgame, and a tough way to lose. We headed back to San Antonio that night.

○   ○   ○

Later that season, on March 31, we were back at home in San Antonio playing against the Sacramento Kings. My cousins were at the game, and as the first half progressed I could tell something wasn't right. I remember looking into the stands and seeing the expressions on their faces—a combination of shock, sadness, anger. I knew them so well they didn't have to say a word.

When the buzzer sounded at the end of the second quarter I quickly weaved my way back to the locker room. Given Dad's health situation, I was always on high alert in those days. Normally, I would put my phone away in my locker before a game and wouldn't look at it again until I got out of the showers after the game. But back then I always checked it at halftime, just in case anybody tried to reach me with an update about the Big Dog. I raced to my stall and pulled out my phone, not knowing what to expect but expecting the worst. There were a handful of text messages and a news alert, all saying the same thing: Nipsey Hussle had been shot outside his storefront on Slauson Avenue in Crenshaw, about ten miles north of Compton. That was the *last* thing I was expecting.

Nip was an influential figure in the local hip-hop community whose career I'd followed closely growing up. We were close in age, and as I was making my rise in the sports world he was making a name for himself in the rap game. His mixtapes were legendary in our neck of the woods, and he was finally breaking through to the mainstream, nominated for a Grammy just a month before the shooting. But by then his biggest impact had nothing to do with music. Nip grew up, like me, surrounded by the Crips in south L.A. He was a member of the Rollin' 60s Crips, and he knew as well as anybody the dangers of that life. But our relationship had nothing to do with the streets. Now, as we were older, Nip had repositioned himself as a builder of communities, not a destroyer. His clothing store on Slauson, called Marathon, generated money that Nip put back into the neighborhood, providing safe community programs for youth and other essentials for families in need.

Only two weeks earlier, Nip and I had had dinner in L.A. to talk about life and the environments we grew up in, and what we could do to help change the course for future generations. Nip started from nothing, but he was so determined to make something not just of himself but of his hometown. We talked about different ways we could give back. He was reaching out to high-profile people like me with hugely ambitious plans to buy back properties in the neighborhoods where we were raised—I'm talking about purchasing entire blocks of houses, renovating them to raise their value, and giving them back to the people. Nip was on some real Robin Hood shit, except he didn't have to rob nobody and was set on doing things the right way. We talked about the power of our platforms, and how we can use our voices to contribute something beyond music or basketball. Nip told me I was already doing that with the way I was inviting people, from our community and others, to think and talk about their mental health.

In the locker room I finished reading up on Nipsey's shooting, destroyed by the thought that even when he was on the up-and-up, he still couldn't escape the threat of violence that hung over the neighborhood. But growing up it felt like people were being shot every day, then wearing their wounds proudly like battle scars. I figured Nip had caught a bullet in the leg or something. He'd be all right. I laced up my sneakers and headed back out for the second half. By the time the game ended, Nipsey was dead. It turned out he'd been shot ten times, murdered in broad daylight in front of his shop by a fellow ex–gang member he grew up with.

I couldn't believe what I was hearing. Instantly, I felt transported back to high school, when people I knew seemed to drop like flies everywhere around me. It had been years and years—not since Davian's killing in my senior year at Compton High—since I felt this. The feeling was powerlessness. Hopelessness. A pending and inevitable crush of sadness and destruction that you knew was coming but could do nothing to stop.

With each year I'd been in the NBA, I had thought those days were in the rearview. Mindless killings. Loved ones buried or behind bars. The types of losses that I had no choice but to experience on a regular basis simply weren't a part of my day-to-day life anymore. They'd been replaced by a different kind of loss—like a close teammate traded away, or a pivotal game dropped at the buzzer. Those losses were sad, of course, and they take their own toll, but they're not life-and-death. And I could explain something like a friend getting traded: There are too many players at his position, or the team is trying to offload salary commitments, whatever. It's the losses I couldn't explain that hurt the most. Like why somebody would walk up to Nip in front of his store, where the proceeds went back into our community, and fire ten bullets into him.

○ ○ ○

We were a decent team my first season in San Antonio. We had a good number of established veterans like myself, Rudy, Aldridge, Pau Gasol, and my old pre-draft training partner in Oakland, Patty Mills. We finished the season with just under fifty wins and pushed the Denver Nuggets and Nikola Jokic to seven games in a hard-fought first-round series, but we ultimately came up short.

I was planning to get away in July—to Montana, the spot along the riverbank—and was enjoying the time with my family until then, watching the rest of the playoffs unfold from my spot on the couch. I watched the Raptors make their run toward the Finals, feeling more conflicted with each round they won. In the championship series versus the Golden State Warriors, Toronto was leading 3–2 with a chance to clinch the title on a Thursday night in June.

I was in L.A., hanging at home that night alone, unsure what to do with myself. I wanted to get out of the house, so I went over to a friend's place. Everybody in the crib was watching the game. For the life of me I didn't want that TV to be on. While they all watched, I paced the room, or put my face down in my phone looking for any distraction I could find. When Toronto won the game, finally bringing home the first championship in team history, I sent Kyle, Norm Powell, Serge Ibaka, Fred VanVleet, and Pascal Siakam—everybody I had played with over there—a text message. It read: "You deserve it and I'm happy for you. Enjoy this. Have fun." I knew they were all back in the locker room, celebrating and spraying champagne everywhere—a scene I had envisioned for ten years—and was genuinely surprised when, to a man, they all responded to me right away. That really meant a lot.

It also meant the world when, during his postgame interview with ESPN, Kyle gave me a shout-out. The way I saw it, this was *his* moment and he didn't have to do that for me. But he did, because that's the kind of guy Kyle is. Later on in the night we had a video call. He was so elated, beyond happy, and despite being in so much pain myself, it helped seeing my best friend enjoying what he had worked so hard for. But I won't lie, it took some time before I could truly let go and just be happy for him and for the fans up in Canada. I saw the parade they had, with more than a million people partying along the streets of Toronto, and it crushed me not to have been a part of seeing things through and celebrating a championship together. For weeks I was riding an emotional roller-coaster. Confusion, sadness, frustration, everything all at once. Eventually a new emotion emerged: acceptance. *It is what it is,* I thought. It was what it was.

CHAPTER 15

January 26, 2020. The Raptors were back in San Antonio. It was still a big game, but a lot of the hype and attention that came with our last matchup in San Antonio—my first time playing Toronto since the trade—had faded. The Raptors were the defending champs but Kawhi had left the team after one season and they were in the process of handing the keys over to Freddie and Pascal. Our team, meanwhile, was struggling to find our footing and were fighting just to make the playoffs. In November, we had a particularly rough stretch. We were playing awful and lost eight games in a row. I remember Pop calling me once after we'd lost to Portland, on his way home from the game. "Man, I'm sorry I brought you here, DeMar," he said. "I really thought we'd be better." But we were turning it around since the New Year and showing signs of life.

I arrived at the AT&T Center for the Toronto game about two hours before tip-off, parked my ride in the players' lot underneath the arena, and headed toward the locker room. I was walking through a hallway, checking up on messages on my phone when a ton of messages and news alerts began popping up. I couldn't believe what I was reading: *Kobe Bryant dies in helicopter crash.* I felt my legs buckling underneath me. I leaned my back against the concourse wall for support, but I slouched over and slid to the ground. I thought it might be some fucked-up joke. "That shit ain't true," I responded to the friends and family texting me with the news. I was in denial. I kept reading the reports and slowly reality set in.

Kobe and I had remained close throughout my career. He never stopped making himself available to me, and I never stopped turning to him for advice, feedback, or inspiration. Kobe was my basketball hero, and I watched in amazement with all the other hoop fans around the world as his career came to a close, when he dropped 60 points in his final NBA game at thirty-seven years old, hobbling on an injured foot but coming through in the clutch like he always had so he could go out with a win. I watched how, in retirement, he transitioned from basketball to other pursuits and made that shit look seamless—whether it was publishing innovative books for young adults, doing media, or winning an Academy Award for *Dear Basketball,* a short film he produced. I watched how he poured his heart and soul into developing programs for girls' basketball through his Mamba Academy. His daughter Gianna, who was thirteen years old, was exploding onto the scene and there was buzz around L.A. that she was gonna be the next great one, that Kobe's hoops legacy was going to carry on with her in the WNBA. Shit, it was only a month or so earlier that I was talking to Kobe about getting Diar into the Mamba Academy. She was just about to turn eight, which was the youngest age she could be to join. "Kob', my girl loves basketball, man, as soon as she's old enough I'm gonna send her to you. I want you to get her right, man." He laughed and sounded legitimately excited by the idea. When I read that Gianna was on the helicopter and died alongside her dad, my heart broke. I could feel the tears streaming down my face.

I stood up and, like a zombie, waded toward the locker room. I didn't say nothing to nobody. I just stared down at my feet. *What the fuck,* was all I could think. Growing up, I'd encountered this feeling plenty of times before. I'd lost people who were close to me in the blink of an eye, with no warning. But with the exception of Nip, those days felt like a lifetime ago. When I reached my locker stall, I collapsed into a chair and kept my gaze to the ground. A few moments later, Coach Pop entered the room. He was crying, too. Pop made a beeline to my locker and gave me a hug, squeezing me tightly. He had his own relationship with Kobe, years of playoff battles that forged a mutual respect amongst champions, but he also knew how close Kobe and I were and how much he meant to me. None of us could grasp what was happening. Obviously nobody saw it coming. He flew everywhere by helicopter. Kobe would famously take a chopper from his house to the Lakers' practice facility to beat the L.A. traffic. The more I read, the more fucked-up it all became. Kobe was flying above the 101 freeway in L.A. along with Gianna and seven other passengers—parents and teammates from her basketball team—on their way from a practice. It was a rare gray and cloudy day, rain drizzling and winds gusting. The helicopter crashed into a hillside in Calabasas, where I live. The accident took place two exits from my house. My property overlooks the sandy hills and canyons. From my backyard I can see the crash site.

After Pop hugged me he grabbed my hands and told me I didn't have to play in the game that night against Toronto. It was the first night of a back-to-back, and the next night we were scheduled to play Chicago. I didn't think about it for long: I played in the game that night—Kobe would have wanted me to—but it was one of the toughest outings I've had. It felt impossible to focus on anything else. We wanted to do something to honor Kobe, so before the game, both teams decided we were going to each begin the game by holding the ball for twenty-four seconds in honor of his jersey number. The rest of the game is just a blur.

The funeral was two weeks later in downtown Los Angeles. Helicopters filled the sky and there were flashing cameras and people everywhere. Twenty thousand people filled the Staples Center for a memorial. It was like Kobe's death blanketed the whole city with sadness. Seeing the reaction to his death from all corners of the world, people from all walks of life, put into perspective the impact that Kobe had on the world. I was just in awe of the steady parade of incredible figures—from basketball royalty like Bill Russell, Michael Jordan, Kareem Abdul-Jabbar, and Diana Taurasi to Beyoncé and Alicia Keys, who both performed. (I got goosebumps when Keys played Beethoven's *Moonlight Sonata* on the piano during the ceremony—a song Kobe loved to play on the piano himself.) I was amazed by how many people he had affected, all in one place.

I flew from the funeral back to San Antonio (we had a game the next night) on a private plane with Coach Pop, Rudy Gay, Tony Parker, Tim Duncan, and Manu Ginobili. It had been a long day and the atmosphere was heavy, as you can imagine. As the plane took off, Pop asked us if we'd been reading the news. "You know about this virus thing, right?" he asked. Pop was always in tune with what was happening outside of basketball and was very plugged into world events. Whether it was protests in Hong Kong or wildfires in California, Pop was always talking about what was going on around us. On this flight he kept talking about a virus that was spreading all over. How it was incredibly contagious and spread quickly and effortlessly, and that scientists hadn't developed any way to treat it yet, let alone to stop the spreading. The whole flight home, Pop was going off about this looming threat. "I don't think you get it, this is a serious matter," he said. We were giving him a hard time and just laughed him off. "Classic Pop," one of the guys said. "You watch too much TV."

○ ○ ○

A stranger in a mask and wearing a full-body hazmat suit slaps a wristband onto my right arm. Then another masked stranger leads me to a massive room and places me in a plastic folding chair. "Look up," the stranger says. They unwrap a giant swab from its packaging and shove it into each of my nostrils, thank me for my patience, and send me upstairs to my hotel room on the campus of the Disney World resort in Lake Buena Vista, Florida, where I'm told I can't, under any circumstances, leave for the next forty-eight hours. It's July 7, normally the early stretch of the off-season, when I'm typically in the wilderness or on a remote beach somewhere. But nothing felt "normal" these days. The NBA's grand experiment—the Bubble—was off and running.

A few months earlier, on March 11, I'm sitting in the house I was renting in San Antonio, watching a game between the Oklahoma City Thunder and the Utah Jazz. The tip-off was delayed when Jazz center Rudy Gobert tested positive for COVID-19, the virus Pop had warned us about on the plane ride back from Kobe's funeral. COVID was still a mystery. We didn't know how to treat it and didn't know how serious it might be. (Within two years, more than a million Americans would die from it.) Ten days earlier, the NBA had sent out a memo to teams, warning us to take precautions. But after Gobert's positive test, the NBA wasn't taking chances. Before the game even began, team doctors rushed the court with the news and the league ended up calling off the game altogether. In all my years of being in the league, and a lifetime of following sports, I had never seen anything like that. I watched it unfold on my TV and, literally, the moment I saw the fans leaving their seats I called one of our assistant coaches, Will Hardy, who is now the head coach of the Jazz.

"Can I go back home to L.A. tonight?"

The night before, we'd played Dallas in what was supposed to be the first game of a five-game home stand. But the writing was on the wall. On several text threads, there was talk about more games being postponed. I figured there was no way we were going to be playing ball anytime soon, so I chartered a plane and flew home that night. What I hadn't considered was that, from the moment I landed in Los Angeles, I would be spending the next two months stuck at the house.

By the next morning, the NBA had suspended the entire season, and other sports leagues followed suit. When I heard that the league was planning to restart the season by transforming Disney World into a world-class hoops facility, it sounded wild. I was skeptical at first, but the more I learned, the more it seemed like they could pull it off. The resort already had a sports complex with multiple arenas and several hotels to house the players and team staff, and there were going to be strict protocols in place—including restricting who was allowed in and out of "the Bubble"—to help keep us safe from getting (and spreading) COVID. I missed hooping so badly that I was down to give it a try.

Before heading to Florida, I had to go back to San Antonio for two weeks and undergo COVID testing every day while self-isolating, meaning I was strictly going back and forth between my crib and the practice court, and nowhere else. I followed the rules—I didn't want to be the one who spread COVID among my teammates and their families. Once I reached the practice court, we never had our full squad, because they were restricting how many people were allowed on the court at once.

So by the time we arrived at the Bubble, I guess you could say we were already used to the protocols and regular testing. Bubble life was so goddamn dull. It was just terrible, in all facets. For the most part, we were stuck in our hotel rooms, watching TV or hanging out on the balcony. Other players found creative ways to pass the time. They'd fish in the man-made lakes on the property, and at night a bunch of them formed a wine club where they'd meet up in the lobby of one of the hotels. I didn't really take part in any of that. I spent more of the time on my balcony. I used to love when it rained, you know that Florida downpour where the skies empty and rain pounds down for twenty minutes or so until the sun comes out. I would sit on the balcony for hours waiting for the rain, thinking, *All this just to play basketball?*

I took advantage of all the downtime in the Bubble by continuing to talk about mental health on a public stage. I was asked if I wanted to do a co-interview alongside Olympic swimmer Michael Phelps, who was probably the highest-profile athlete before me to talk about battling depression and the pressures of life in the public eye. I jumped at the opportunity. In the interview, which was done virtually from my hotel room at Disney World, we went back and forth sharing our experiences. I talked about growing up in an atmosphere where you felt you needed to keep your feelings bottled inside, and how important it was for me to have found an outlet for that pent-up emotion in basketball. Phelps talked about ADHD and the emotional roller-coaster ride he'd been on all of his life, how scared he was to be vulnerable after hiding himself in his sport and becoming one of the greatest Olympians of all time. It was powerful to hear. As I listened I kept thinking how different we were—two people from completely different walks of life, a white guy from Baltimore whose dad was a state trooper and a Black dude from Compton, growing up surrounded by gangs and violence—yet our experiences with mental health were universal and brought us together.

When it was finally time to play ball in the Bubble, the atmosphere was bizarre. Playing an NBA game in a gym with nobody there was definitely a new experience. They had fans appearing on giant screens surrounding the court, like we were playing in front of a backdrop of the world's largest Zoom call. Fake cheering and arena noise was piped in on speakers. It was different. The shine wore off quickly. I'd gotten spoiled spending the previous months at home with my girls, and I missed them so much. There was so much happening in the world that the last place I wanted to be was on the opposite end of the country, eating take-out food in a hotel room alone for days on end. It wasn't just COVID that gripped our attention. The brutal murder of George Floyd by a Minnesota police officer back in May had set off a firestorm of uprising and demonstrations. The NBA was using its platform to spread awareness, painting "Black Lives Matter" across the Bubble courts, and the players were eager to promote the movement, appearing at protests and marches around the country, like one in Compton that I took part in. On August 23, Jacob Blake was shot and killed by a police officer in Wisconsin, and the teams in the Bubble boycotted their game out of protest. I was proud to be part of a group that was willing to take a stand.

I was already back home by then. Our time in the Bubble lasted eight games before we were eliminated. It seemed like a crazy amount of upheaval and work for just eight games, but I love hooping, so looking back, I think it was worth it. But I was happy to be home. The world was in a crisis and I had to be present for my family. Things had been up and down for Kiara and me since our separation. We were separated when the trade from Toronto happened, and when Dad was moved from his room at Cedars-Sinai to a convalescent home, and I felt her absence during those periods of transition. But we were never far apart, and we still felt close throughout that time. We had kids to raise, and Kiara and I were determined to give our girls the best life we possibly could. Their happiness was the most important thing to us, and so we still shared the house and made sure the kids felt like everything was normal, even when it wasn't. My schedule is so hectic and I was already always in and out of town because of my work, so we hoped that things wouldn't feel different for the girls day-to-day. To be honest, I don't think Diar or Mari had any idea what was happening. Whether they did or not, we were doing our best to make it work.

We may have done too good of a job: When I returned from the Bubble, Kiara told me that she was pregnant with our third child, another girl. *That* was unexpected. Despite putting on a brave face for Diar and Mari, we still hadn't really worked on resolving our issues or understanding what was behind them. We hadn't put in the time and effort we needed to rekindle our relationship. Now with a third kid on the way, the girls out of school indefinitely because of COVID, and the whole world seemingly crumbling around us, it didn't exactly feel like that was about to change. Everything was just so out of whack. We decided not to tell anybody about the pregnancy yet. We were too busy trying to teach ourselves how to crawl out of quicksand.

CHAPTER 16

The NBA's Bubble experiment had ended, and the league found a way to return to action for the 2021–22 season—thanks to half-filled arenas due to social distancing, constant testing, and strict rules that limited how much we were able to leave our hotels and be around people outside of our teams.

We were in L.A. just after New Year's to play a pair of games against the Lakers and the Clippers. Dad couldn't be there—before the Lakers game I received the news that he had to be taken from his convalescent home to the hospital. Nobody was quite sure what happened—the leading theory was that he'd eaten something spicy that upset his stomach. Next thing you know he had acid reflux and was feeling sick. Turns out it wasn't something he ate: Once he was examined at the hospital, the doctors determined that he had suffered several strokes and would need to be admitted.

COVID restrictions were in full force, and none of our family was allowed inside the hospital to visit Dad. Over the next few weeks I got updates on his health status. It was getting real bad. The doctors explained to me how basically everything was starting to fail him. His kidneys were on the brink of disaster. Blood clots were developing everywhere. It was just issue after issue. I wanted desperately to be by his side at the hospital, but it wasn't an option. Not even a week later, I was back on the road, this time in Minnesota, when I got a call from the hospital letting me know that they had no choice but to put him on a ventilator to assist with breathing. I flew home that night. I knew I wasn't going to be able to see him, but I wanted to be there for Mom. She was holding on best as she could—there was nobody stronger than Mom—but to know Dad was suffering and not be able to hold his hand, or kiss his cheek and let him know everything was going to be all right, that ate away at her.

I was home for a couple days before I had to rejoin the team. Before I left, I arranged for Mom to come to the house to live with us for a while, and I made a plan with the hospital to set up a Zoom call between Mom and Dad. We set up a computer in the living room, with a comfortable reclining chair in front of it for Mom to sit in. I stood behind her as we made our first Zoom call with Dad—the first of many. When the camera turned on, the image on the other end was a shock. Dad was unconscious, unable to speak, hooked up to his breathing machine with all sorts of tubes and wires attached to him. "Hey, darling, how are you?" Mom asked him. He didn't respond. He couldn't respond. That didn't stop Mom. She kept chatting his ear off, talking to him as if he was talking back and they were deep in conversation. Hours passed like that, Mom talking to Dad like everything was normal, telling him about her day, and what their grandchildren learned in school that week, gossiping about the neighbors and anything else that came into her mind. Six hours passed. Seven hours passed.

Eventually, the medical team had to step in and gently tell my mom that Dad needed to sign off so that he could get some much-needed treatment.

Every day for two weeks straight, Mom would talk to Dad like that. Some days, my older brother, Jermaine, would come over and join her. I think it was too hard for my sister, Vanessa, to see her father in that state.

When I saw the man on the computer screen, I knew that wasn't my dad. My dad was a strong, proud man. The face on the screen looked frightened and defeated. After a couple of weeks he began to open his eyes, and every now and then you'd see him lift a hand or make some sort of movement. That was big progress, we were told, but when I looked closely at him I saw the writing on the wall. I could tell from his eyes. The fire was gone from them. But I kept those thoughts to myself. I could tell that my mom and siblings were still holding on to hope that he would battle his way out of this. He was getting the best medical treatment possible and, my dad being the stubborn guy he was, you knew he'd try to claw his way back. He'd done it so many times before.

One day, we were on the video call with Dad and he spoke for the first time since returning to the hospital.

"I want," he told us, "to get out of here."

But the words could barely escape his mouth. All the strength had been sapped from his voice. By then he was too scared to run and too weak to fight. I could see how badly he was hurting.

I was in Charlotte when he passed. We had just wrapped up a game against the Hornets, and we learned that our next two games had been postponed due to a COVID outbreak on one of the opposing teams. Back in San Antonio there were ice storms and flights were being grounded, so we were stuck in the Charlotte hotel for two days while waiting out the storm. I was in my room, alone, one night when I got the call from the hospital informing me that Dad passed away in his sleep. I called Brian Wright, the Spurs general manager, and told him the news.

"I have to fly home tonight," I told him.

I guess Brian shared the news with Pop, because literally two minutes after I hung up the phone there was a knock on my door. I picked myself up off the bed and opened it. Pop walked in. He didn't say anything—sometimes there's nothing to say—he just wrapped his arms around me and squeezed tightly. Then he sat on the edge of the bed and stayed beside me for I don't even know how long. Hours, I'm sure. He didn't have to do that, and it just speaks to this tremendous compassion and empathy that Pop carries with him everywhere he goes. And it's not just Pop—the whole organization operates like that. The respect and care they showed me during my two seasons in San Antonio blew me away. A lot of teams wouldn't act that way. It meant so much to me, especially after how things ended in Toronto.

I kept picturing Mom and Dad on their Zoom calls, the gaunt, empty man on the computer screen, alone in a hospital room during his most vulnerable days. Because of the whole COVID situation, his loved ones hadn't seen him in person for months. That was the most painful part. It still hurts so much to think about: The old man had to go by himself, with nobody by his side.

I flew out from Charlotte on a 6 A.M. flight and spent the rest of the day dealing with everything that had to be dealt with—the paperwork and other administrative stuff, going through photos—all those faded faces—and taking care of Mom, who was struggling to accept that Dad was gone. As much as it hurt when he passed, I felt a strange sense of relief. In a way it was like he'd always been preparing me for this moment. I thought back to times on the court at Wilson Park in Compton, to our spirited games of one-on-one, Dad showing no mercy on me as I did whatever I could to find a way to beat him and earn his respect.

"You know, DeMar, there will be a time when I'm not going to be here for you," he'd say as I wiped away my tears. "One day I'm gonna be gone, and you've got to be able to handle things for the family."

I was ready. *All right, I got this,* I told myself. *Everything you've taught me for the last thirty years, I understand now.* In those days following his death, it was like all of his lessons were being repeated in my head. To be accountable, to work hard, and to appreciate what you have. He taught me that you didn't need to be loud to command respect. I soaked up whatever I could. Dad wasn't perfect. He made a lot of mistakes along the way. We all do. He was old-school, locking me in the closet and showing the kind of tough love he was raised on, but that I wouldn't dream of using with my own children. He had two children from a previous marriage, and he was always present and supportive in their lives. He would never turn his back on his kids. I can still hear his voice talking to C-Farr or any of my other coaches—*"You keep pushing him. My boy still has more to give."* Dad saw something special in me long before I ever did. He pushed me, even when I couldn't stand it, because he knew my potential. What he saw in me, he wanted me to see in myself. My siblings used to always tell people that Dad just *loved* DeMar. And I felt that from him. He was my harshest critic and my biggest cheerleader. After he died, I got a tattoo of his face across my shoulder so that Dad and I will always be together.

I was the protector of my family now, and it was like the universe was testing me. One night, a few months after Dad passed, I was in the basement, getting work done on the tattoo. It was around 7 P.M. and Kiara was upstairs with the girls. Mari was already down for bed, and Diar was in the kids' playroom beside the kitchen, getting some "me time" before her bedtime. Out of nowhere there was a snap—like a lightning strike—and the basement was in total darkness. I pivoted my way through the pitch black toward the stairwell and flicked a light switch. Nothing. The power in the whole house was out. As I headed to the fuse box, I heard screams coming from upstairs. It was Diar. I dashed up the stairs and saw a young shirtless white guy running through the sliding glass door into our backyard. I chased him and saw him disappear down the driveway into our cul-de-sac. I thought about sprinting to catch him but Diar was inside. I ran back to the house. I didn't know if anyone else was in the house. I grabbed a baseball bat from the front closet and started going through the house room by room, my back firmly against the wall and the bat against my chest like it was a rifle and I was a Navy SEAL. Kiara heard the commotion and called 911 as I finished checking the rest of the house.

When the cops arrived, they looked at the security video. Someone had come onto our property, cut the power line with shears, and broken in through a sliding door in the back. When Diar spotted him, he told her to be quiet. That's when she screamed, and once he heard me, he scurried off like a cockroach when you turn the lights on. It turned out that not only was he alone, but he had gotten the wrong house. Apparently he had driven all the way from North Dakota with a plan to break into the home of my next-door neighbor, Kylie Jenner. Word is he admitted it all to the police a few hours later, after security caught him trying to sneak back into our gated housing community for the second time later that night.

○ ○ ○

With a new wave of COVID hitting America with full force, we had no choice but to postpone Dad's funeral. With the paperwork and everything out of the way, I didn't know what to do with myself and didn't want to wallow around the house trying to process my pain. I needed an outlet. So I went back to work. Within a week I was back on the road, joining the team in Oklahoma City. Looking back, I wish I had given myself more time to grieve, more time with my family, but basketball was my comfort food and I needed to eat.

We finally had the funeral about a month later. It had been three and a half months from the time my dad got sick and had to return to the hospital to the day of his funeral. During that time, none of his loved ones had seen him in person. I flew into Los Angeles on the morning of the funeral service.

On the flight over, I was breathing heavy and tried to catch my breath. I tried to close my eyes and get some rest, but I couldn't sleep. It felt like every time my eyelids touched I'd begin to hear the sound of crashing waves. I opened my eyes quickly to avoid falling into a nightmare. It was a particularly crazy time for all of us and I'd been going through a lot outside of Dad's health and passing. It had been a long time since the NBA's Bubble, when I was cloistered in Disney World with no physical contact with my family, but I felt just as isolated in the months that followed, moving from one hotel room to another, not being around anybody outside of basketball. I was suffering. Talking about my mental health had been liberating, but it was hardly some magic elixir to make me feel better, to wipe away a lifetime of pain and sadness. I just wanted to be there for Dad and the family and to not be a distraction during that time, so as I found myself in another emotional valley, I kept quiet about it. Meanwhile, Kiara was still pregnant with our third daughter, and we still hadn't shared the news. She was so far along in her pregnancy that she wasn't able to attend the funeral.

All of my cousins and members of Mom's family were there to pay their respects, along with several members of the Compton community that Dad had made an impact on, whether it was with his work at City Hall or by coaching youth football. I was touched, but not surprised, at how many people were there to express love and respect for the old man.

The night of the funeral, Kiara's water broke. We rushed to the hospital and found out that our daughter was ready to enter the world. The same day we buried Dad, our third daughter was born. The circle of life, man. It can't hit you any harder than that. We named our girl Dayah—as in, she was born on the "day-of" Dad's funeral.

　　　　・　　　・　　　・

My family was growing quickly. Dayah joined her sisters and it felt like she had been with us from the beginning. Diar is curious by nature and values alone time like her daddy, and Mari is happiest when the spotlight is on her, but Dayah is unlike either of them. She's a total live wire—as soon as she learned to walk, it was game over. The girl don't stop. I'd come home from workout sessions, and my legs would just about cramp up as I chased after her around the house trying to keep tabs on her. I thought Mari was the life of the party . . . and then I met Dayah.

Meanwhile, Kiara and I were trying to make our partnership work so that, at the very least, the kids felt as though they had two stable parents in their lives, even if I had to be on the road so much and the seatbelt sign in our relationship felt like it was always on due to turbulence.

Our relationship still feels like a process, to be honest. Naturally, there are good days and bad, and although it felt like we were finally making progress after Dayah came into this world, our family dynamics were only beginning to settle. It felt like we were in a good place. And then I found out that I had a son on the way with another woman. I was headed home from a game in San Antonio, not long after Dad's passing, when I got the news. It wasn't planned, or anything I saw coming, and as much as I loved being a dad I knew this wouldn't be easy to navigate.

It took me a long time to work up the nerve to tell Kiara. When I did, I felt like I was at the free-throw line in Game 7 of the Finals with zero seconds left on the clock in a tie game—only at least that was a scenario I'd been preparing myself for practically all my life. To tell my longtime partner, the mother of our three daughters, that I was going to have a child with another woman? I hadn't practiced that one. When I told Kiara, she took it hard. How could she not? It was hard for everybody and a difficult topic to talk about. But if there's anything I'd learned in recent years, since coming forward with my battles with depression, it's that talking about it—"it" being anything, from your mental well-being to the bomb I was dropping on Kiara—is the first and often most important step toward resolution. Of course, that didn't make it any easier.

Fatherhood never scared me. From Grandma, to my parents and cousins, I always wanted to be in the role of caregiver and provider. When Kiara and I had our girls, I loved how they brought out a softer side of me that I'd had to keep repressed growing up in a place where that was viewed as a sign of weakness. But deep down, I was always terrified of having a son. I loved being a girl dad, kissing boo-boos better. I felt like I couldn't be that way with my son, that I would need to be hard on him like my dad was on me. In November 2021, as soon as my son, Zino, was born, all of that went out the window. I love my boy and shower him with the same kind of love my girls get. The situation is still playing itself out. Zino is a sweet, quiet, curious kid, and he soaks things in quickly. I see him every Wednesday, and we spend the day together from sunup to sundown. We'll go visit Grandma, or hang out with his half-sisters, and I treasure and appreciate our time together.

Six months after Zino was born, Kiara and I welcomed our fourth daughter, Reezen, into the world. Life is complicated. So far, Reezen is the spectator of the group and is still coming into her own, which is amazing to watch. Her favorite toy these days is a Rubik's Cube that her big sister Diar gave to her. Reezen is just taking it all in. In a way, we all are, taking things one day at a time. It's tough to say exactly where Kiara's and my relationship is at, because it still feels very fluid. From those innocent days on the campus of USC, to planting roots in another country, to managing our family dynamics, we've been through the emotional wringer together. But we keep focused on making sure our kids are good. I hope the rest will fall into place.

CHAPTER 17

"I wanna see you win one."

In the summer before Zino was born, I was at the crib by myself, sprawled on the couch after my second workout of the day, watching a Finals game between the Phoenix Suns and Milwaukee Bucks, when I got the text from LeBron.

The final year of the five-year contract I had signed with the Raptors back in 2016, which officially felt like a lifetime ago, had just wrapped. My second and final season in San Antonio had been, in one sense, frustrating. For the first time in eight years, I missed the playoffs, and I badly wanted an opportunity to compete for a championship, especially having felt so agonizingly close during the end of my time in Toronto. On the other hand, I wouldn't have traded my experience in San Antonio for the world. I felt welcomed and supported by a world-class organization. I'm grateful that I was playing for the Spurs during such a tough stretch, between my very public mental-health journey and the passing of my dad, and to have formed a relationship with a person like Coach Pop. Two years later, I was playing against the Spurs when I scored my 20,000th point in the NBA and Pop immediately called a timeout so that I could acknowledge the fans cheering for me, and soak in the moment. To be one of only fifty players in league history to join the 20,000-point club is a legit milestone. And Pop's gesture, like so many others, spoke volumes to me.

But the writing was on the wall, and my time in San Antonio had drawn to a close. I knew they wanted to rebuild the roster and bring in young players—which meant competing for a championship wasn't in the cards anytime soon—and I still had so much to give on the court. At the end of the season, the Spurs told me they would hook up a sign-and-trade deal (a scenario where a team re-signs a player to a new deal immediately before trading him, as a creative way of working around the NBA's salary-cap rules) or whatever else they could do to help me wind up on the team of my choice.

I always wanted to play for the same team throughout my career, to be a consistent presence for a franchise and a city, like Kobe to the Lakers and Michael to the Bulls. I truly believed that I would be that person for the Raptors, and it's why, both times my contract was up when I was with Toronto, I signed an extension with no hesitation. I didn't choose to be traded. Now, for the first time in my career, I was entering the summer as a free agent, free to choose where I would land next.

In Los Angeles, meanwhile, LeBron had delivered a championship to the Lakers in 2020 inside the NBA's Disney World bubble. But now, one year later, he was watching the Finals at home like I was, after the Lakers were knocked out by the Suns in the first round. 'Bron was looking to bolster the roster and add talent alongside him and Anthony Davis, and knew I was entering free agency.

When I got the text—*I wanna see you win one*—I knew what the implication was. *Well, shit, so do I,* I thought. "Let's figure out a way to make it happen," I wrote back. The Lakers instantly became my first option. Playing for the team I grew up in awe of, with a serious shot at winning it all? Sign me up.

Once the Finals wrapped and the free-agency period began, I went over to 'Bron's house in the Brentwood neighborhood in L.A. We sat on his patio and ate a meal by a long and narrow rectangular pool, a strategically placed awning shielding us from the summer sun. I've known LeBron since I was seventeen, when I first attended one of his camps. Being one of the top players there, I was able to connect with him and talk about hoops and life, and we maintained a relationship from there. There's a mutual respect that 'Bron and I share. He's a real one. We both are. Like me, he never had it easy growing up. He was raised in Akron, living with a single mother in an impoverished, dangerous environment that forces you to grow up faster than any kid should have to. I knew what that felt like, that loss of innocence. But I was impressed by the way he was able to emerge from that upbringing and make the most out of life. I'm not sure if people would expect it, but the reality is LeBron is just a big kid. He likes to joke around all the time and enjoy life. He's a cool dude who, despite being one of the most famous people on the planet, somehow manages to remain just a normal guy in a lot of ways.

That respect between us carried over to the court, and there was never any bad blood from our playoff battles. Don't get me wrong—it was painful to have the season end in heartbreak year after year, losing to the same player and the same team—but I never took nothing personal from that. 'Bron was doing what he does best.

As we sat and ate, we talked strategy, writing down potential plays and offensive sets on nearby napkins. We broke down the Lakers' existing roster and discussed what types of players we could add who would be the best fit around LeBron, Anthony

Davis, and me. I left 'Bron's house thrilled for the next chapter. To wear the purple and gold that I'd watched streak across the TV screen growing up; to work and live in the same city as my children and not have to spend so many nights away, missing them so badly that I can't sleep; to be a short drive away from Mom's house, not having to charter flights around the country in order to check in on her like I had to with Dad . . .

I took my family to Mexico for a short vacation soon after that. As we left Los Angeles, I felt a sense of calm washing over me. The universe works in wonderful ways, I thought. The next episode of my career was set.

○ ○ ○

I woke up in Mexico on the morning of August 6 to the news: The Lakers had traded for Russell Westbrook, the all-star point guard.

Immediately the reality sunk in. *Goddamn, how am I going to go there now?* My deal to the Lakers was done, or so I figured, and I was expecting to officially ink a contract within the next few days. But the Westbrook news changed all that. Russ joined L.A. with two years left on a contract that was paying him more than $40 million per season, and it didn't take an astrophysicist to do the math that the Lakers didn't have enough room under the league's salary cap anymore to be able to sign me.

At first it was like a punch to the gut. The stars had all aligned, only to disappear completely.

I really tried to make it work with the Lakers, but now I'm glad it didn't happen. If I'm honest with myself, I wasn't in it for the right reasons. I wanted to be home, be close to my mom. I had my son on the way and was thinking about how I was going to manage that. I felt at a crossroads and didn't know which direction to go. It felt like the shit was hitting the fan. When it did, I figured, at least this time I'd be home. Put it all together, and basketball was like the fourth or fifth reason behind my decision-making. That didn't feel right. So it was back to the drawing board.

I looked around at my options, at the teams that still had the interest—and cap space—to sign me. One of the teams that fit the bill: the Chicago Bulls. The year before, Chicago had traded for Nik Vučević—"Vooch"—my old college teammate at USC. We'd stayed close since our college days, keeping in touch on a regular basis, texting memes and jokes to each other all the time, and it was cool to watch him progress into an all-star-caliber center. When Vooch got to Chicago, his first game in a Bulls uniform was in San Antonio against me and the Spurs. Before tip-off, while I was still in the layup line, Vooch pulled me aside.

"Hey, I know you're a free agent this summer . . ." he said, raising his eyebrows.

"Man, we'll see what's what," I told him.

Fast-forward to the summertime, and suddenly Chicago was looking more and more appealing. I already had a friend on the team in Vooch, plus I had an existing relationship with the Bulls GM, Marc Eversley, who had been on the Raptors' staff and came to watch me work out at Merritt College in Oakland. He'd been a big part of Toronto drafting me all those years ago. The Bulls hadn't made the postseason in five years, but Marc was trying to change the ship's course—trading for a player of Vooch's ability was a clear sign—and I knew his intention was to win now. I called Marc right away from Mexico—things were happening very fast in this off-season, with the Westbrook trade showing how one move can disrupt the whole landscape, and I didn't want to wait until I was back home.

Marc explained how he wanted to bring me in because except for Vooch, the team were mainly young up-and-coming players, and he thought I could help them turn the corner and get back to the playoffs. The thought of playing for Chicago, putting on the same jersey that MJ wore and competing in the same building as His Airness, was inspiring, but I told Marc that I was worried because the team didn't have a starting point guard, which could stall his plans to be a legit contender in the East. Marc assured me that he was planning to bring somebody in for the job.

The next day Chicago traded for Lonzo Ball, who five years earlier was the NBA's second-overall draft pick. I was all in after that. Lonzo had been caught up in a media firestorm when he entered the league—it seemed like every day there was a new story about Lonzo and his dad, who was front and center touting his son's abilities and starring in a reality TV show about his family. It all overshadowed what Lonzo could do on the court, and so I don't think most people—fans, at least—realize how good he is. Sharing the court with him, as a teammate or opponent, it's impossible to ignore that the dude is *amazing* at running the point. Thirty-five games into his Chicago tenure, Lonzo went down with a knee injury. Two years later, as I write this, he still hasn't returned to the court.

I committed to Chicago, signing a two-year deal, and spent the rest of my summer in L.A., working my ass off. I wanted to be overly prepared for whatever was next and come into the season ready, and better than ever.

          °   °   °

I recognized it all from *The Last Dance*. That, or the dozens—maybe hundreds—of videotapes of Chicago Bulls broadcasts that Dad used to plunk me in front of when I was a little boy, eager to show me what true greatness looked like. When I joined the Bulls, there were signs of Michael Jordan everywhere. More than twenty years after his final season in Chicago, which was chronicled by the Netflix documentary series that everybody and their mother watched during the pandemic, Jordan's presence still hung over every element of the organization.

My first time arriving at the United Center arena in Chicago as a member of the team, I felt like I was stepping into the screen and onto the set of one of my favorite TV shows. Driving down the tunnel and pulling into the players' parking lot, I couldn't believe how familiar it all was. I had seen it all on TV before—Jordan, whose game-winning shots I used to re-create while falling back onto my bed in Compton, arriving at this very same lot in his famous red Corvette, heading into the same locker room I was headed to, to put on the same uniform I was about to wear, ready to do what he did best in front of the same Chicago crowd who were now cheering *my* name. It was a trip, and the feeling of awe and being transported back to my childhood never went away during all my time in Chicago. I mean, how could it? I'll never forget my first game as a Bull during preseason in October. Warming up before the game and looking up into the rafters, I saw MJ's jersey hanging, along with the six championship banners the team won during the Jordan era, and instantly felt his spirit hovering about and a responsibility to perform up to his standard of excellence. (It didn't always work out that way: A few months later, we were down by one with a final shot to take. I got the ball and, just like I'd practiced countless times in my bedroom back on Acacia and on the playground, pulled up for a classic Jordanesque fadeaway jumper to win the game at the buzzer. Airball. It was humbling to try to live up to his standards and fail; I felt so much pressure to be like Mike that watching the ball miss the mesh so badly was a helpful reminder to just be myself.) As I prepared to take the court, I heard a sound swell up in the arena—the single, droning bass note that alerts the crowd and makes way for the synthesizers and dancing guitar riff from the Alan Parsons Project song "Sirius" that famously accompanies players onto the court—and goosebumps blanketed both of my arms. Walking out to that entrance music made every home game feel like the Finals.

As much as it felt like things were lining up when it came to my career, heading into my first season in Chicago I still felt weighed down by the turmoil surrounding me. It had been months since Dad's passing, but the further removed I was from his death, the more guilty I felt for having not necessarily grieved the right way. I wanted to celebrate his life and to give myself time to heal, but instead after he died I just sort of moved on and returned to work like there was nothing else to do. The healing will come through hooping, I told myself. I came home briefly, did what I had to do, supported the people I had to support, and then it was right back to playing. Now that a new season was here in the blink of an eye, it was dawning on me that maybe I had swept away the emotion of it all: losing Dad, raising a growing family while Kiara and I still tried to work through our issues, navigating my career and dealing with the skeletons that still hung in my closet from the Toronto trade. I was scared about how I would make it out alive. My whole life I had been sweeping my feelings away, letting them fester inside until the waves are so powerful that I feel like they're drowning me.

With all the chaos on the outside, I looked forward to finding some peace through hooping and entered the season ready—no, desperate—for a fresh start. That's what my early days in Chicago represented. From the opening tip it was just that. Everything felt different, like a breath of fresh air. I'd been given a new opportunity to lead a team with playoff ambitions, and I had another burst of motivation after reading stories in the media about the Bulls making a mistake by signing me to a three-year contract. (At thirty-two years old, many said, I was past my prime.) I couldn't wait to prove them all wrong.

I used to let all the noise get to me, but I'm learning to rise above it. I'm realizing that it all starts from within. My journey with mental health, finding my voice and encouraging others to find theirs, gave me a self-confidence I hadn't had. I gained so much strength, not just from knowing what I'd overcome to be in this position—entering my thirteenth NBA season—but also from knowing that I was allowed to be vulnerable. Plus with Dad no longer in the picture, I knew I had to be stronger than ever for myself and my family.

It's no wonder my time in Chicago got off to such a good start. I felt energized on the court, electric even. We jumped out to first place in the East at the beginning of the season, and I felt like I had a command over the game like never before. I was breaking records—in November I passed Jordan for the most points scored by a Chicago player in their first sixteen games with the team (Jordan scored 424, I managed 425). By February, I was on a tear and beat a record of Wilt Chamberlain's by scoring 30 points while shooting more than 50 percent from the field in seven straight games. It was a total rejuvenation. At thirty-two years old, I was playing the best basketball of my life. We were winning, I was in MVP talks for the first time in my career, I closed out the All-Star game with the ball in my hands, and I finished the season second in the NBA in scoring. Still, I lay awake at night.

CHAPTER 18

The hardest part of doing what I do is being away from my kids. I've heard teammates say it takes a long time to get used to, but I've never really gotten used to it. When Diar was little, it was a real struggle. Now that she has her siblings, it's easier to swallow when I know that they all have one another. But I still think back to those early days, especially once Diar could talk and she'd pout and say "Daddy, please don't go." That shit broke my heart. I couldn't stand leaving her. I still can't.

At the end of the 2023 season, the Bulls qualified for the "play-in" game—a do-or-die postseason game that the NBA recently added to determine which teams get the last two playoff spots in each conference. And wouldn't you know it, our opponent was the Raptors, with the big game played in Toronto. Diar was only six when we were forced to move out of Toronto, but she remembered her time there well. She remembered her school and her classmates, and the park near our house in Etobicoke. She remembered joining me at the podium after playoff games, and going with her daddy to his office at the Air Canada Centre. In the basement of our home in L.A. is a picture of Diar and me on the sidelines during the dunk contest at the 2016 All-Star weekend in Toronto, and whenever she passes it now, she gets excited and tells whoever is nearby about when she lived in Canada.

Diar is getting more into basketball these days, although I'm conscious not to force the game on her. But I guess you could say she comes by it naturally. Whenever we watch games together, she hammers me with questions. In the weeks leading up to the play-in game, she started hinting that she wanted to go. Being a big sports fan, she understood the magnitude of the game—"win and you're in"—and wanted to be there to cheer me and my team. I told her "No," because Kiara and I didn't want to pull her out of school. But she just kept asking and asking. Two days before the game, I was in Chicago wrapping up practice when I got a call from her. "I *really* want to go, Daddy." I just couldn't say no anymore. I flew to L.A. to pick her up, and the two of us made the trip back to Toronto together.

The play-in game turned out to be a great victory for us that secured us a playoff spot. I'd had been back to Toronto a number of times by then, of course, and as close as I still felt to the city and its fans, I don't travel with the same emotional baggage that I did my first few times back after being traded. But I must admit it felt nice to get such a big win in a place that I had so many feelings wrapped around. The game was close throughout—we only won by 4—but there was a huge discrepancy when it came to free throws, which turned out to be a difference-maker for us. We shot 18 for 22 from the free throw line. The Raptors, on the other hand, managed just 18 for 36, or 50 percent—way below their season average of 76 percent.

After the game, I said a quick hi to familiar faces, like Nav, the Raptors' "superfan," and wished former teammates like Pascal and Freddie a great summer. By the time I got to the locker room, my teammates were howling.

"Man, Diar is *everywhere*," one of them said.

"Your daughter is officially viral!" shouted another.

"What are you talking about?" I asked.

They started pulling out their phones, and sure enough, there it was: clip after clip of my little baby Diar sitting in a seat along the baseline, wearing a Chicago Bulls starter jacket with a giant "D" and her name in rhinestones across the front and "Daddy's Girl" stitched along the left arm, screaming at the top of her lungs during each and every free throw the Raptors shot. Her timing was impeccable, reaching the apex of her high-pitched yell just as the ball was leaving the shooter's hands. Who's to say if she was the reason why Toronto missed so many free throws, but I bet it didn't hurt!

I was proud of her. Not for potentially influencing the outcome of the game, but because I could tell that she was having a blast doing it. It was gratifying to see her coming out of her shell and enjoying herself. Being a big sister with four younger siblings, she has a lot of responsibility thrown at her, and she takes it upon herself to be a role model for her sisters and her half-brother. But there are still times when she gets really quiet and has to have time to herself.

When I watched the video after the game, it was heartwarming to see her get her own moment like that. Diar loved the attention she received from everybody—the Bulls players and staff members were all congratulating her for her part in our big win. "Oh, thank you, thank you, thank you," she said, parading around the locker room with a smile from ear to ear.

Sharing my story has been my own form of therapy. Trying to remember all this stuff and put it in the right order makes it real like nothing else. I'm not done working on myself: In a lot of ways I feel like I've only just begun taking the steps toward healing my wounds. But in opening up and talking about the struggles I've gone through and the pain I've had to overcome just to reach the starting line, I know that I've taken the most important step.

As men, and especially Black men, we don't talk about our mental health enough. We struggle to admit when things aren't okay, even when it's obvious to everybody around us. I've seen how toxic that can become. I've experienced it myself, keeping everything under wraps until your head and heart are full of fire and rage. We need to be able to be vulnerable, to show our weaknesses, and to ask for help when we need it. I still have bad days. But I'm more empowered than ever to keep fighting for the next one.

It's funny—and also sad—that people think just because I'm a successful pro athlete that I can't suffer the same as anybody else. That my physical stature—the size that left me insecure as a kid for being so much bigger than my classmates—and the balance in my bank account somehow make me immune to the challenges of everyday life. Not only do I struggle, but when I do, the whole world sees it. My success is public, just as my failures are. It took me a very long time to accept that fact. It took me even longer to learn to ignore what other people say about me, and to find strength and confidence from within. Talking about my weaknesses helps. Seeing the ways my words and my example can affect people who look up to me has helped even more. I've been blessed to have been given a platform where my words can not only reach a wide audience, but also carry weight. I'm as fucked-up and flawed as the next man. But I will never shy away from the responsibility that's been bestowed on me.

When I first talked about my own battles with depression, I just needed an outlet. But it's become so much more. I've been able to inspire others by showing the courage to open up and admit to the pain I struggle to overcome. I'm helping to break stigmas of what it means to be vulnerable. When people, including my fellow athletes, thank me for opening the door for them to explore their own struggles, or to use their own stage to promote taking care of their mental health, I don't know how to respond. "Humbling" doesn't begin to describe it.

Looking back through these pages makes me feel like I can get through anything. I've been through the toughest of the tough, and have seen the closest people to me never come back again. New Year's never goes by without me thinking about Davian, and everywhere I look I'm reminded of Dad.

I'll never forget where I came from. I can't. Compton is a part of me. I'll always be a part of the community and return whenever I can to provide the same hope and visibility to a younger generation, because I know from experience how inspiring that can be. Compton raised me. It taught me to be resilient, to experience and overcome hardship. Compton provided me with an imagination to explore. I wear my roots like a badge of honor. The good, the bad, I wouldn't be who I am today if it wasn't for what I learned growing up in Compton.

I think about what the next chapter of my life will look like after I retire. I think about the chance to fully engulf myself in fatherhood. I think about decompressing from more than fifteen years of mental, physical, and emotional strain of my career. When I hang it up, there's a good chance you'll see me disappear for a minute as I take a big step back and indulge in the normalcy of life. But I'm not there yet.

People often ask me why I still do what I do. I've accomplished so much on the court and made more money than I know what to do with. Why still spend so much time on the road away from my kids when I miss them so terribly? Why did I spend so much time and effort traveling back home between games to visit Dad in the hospital? Why didn't I just take a leave from work instead? And why return to hooping so soon after he passed? There's an easy answer: Because, like Dad always said, I know I still have more to give on the court.

But the real answer? I still need basketball.

I love the game and appreciate what it's provided. All the wealth in the world don't amount to shit if you can't find peace within yourself. Basketball is where I find peace. Always has been. And these days, that's all I'm looking for. Whether it's in the foothills of Montana, in a boat on a shimmering lake, or in the comfort of my home surrounded by family, I still crave the sense of calm I've been chasing all my life.

I know I'll never be fully removed from my past. To this day, I have close family and friends who are still in Compton, eking out a living in that world with no choice but to take it one day at a time. They're still fending off the sounds of the night.

Some nights, I still feel like I am, too.

It's getting late. The house has gone eerily quiet. I look out my back door and can see a yellow moonbeam splashing across the swimming pool. Before I call it a night, I'll go upstairs, past the mural of Compton painted on the wall behind my couch, and kiss my girls, who are tucked into bed. I'll step outside the back door, feeling the sharp blades of freshly cut grass against the soles of my bare feet, and make my way toward the pool. I'll tell myself to look away, but my eyes will peek up to the right at the hill where Kobe's helicopter crashed, in plain view even after nightfall. I'll look up at the moon, shining bright tonight. These days, if I stare at it long enough, I swear I can see Dad's face in it. Just like the stars, it'll shine again tomorrow.

ACKNOWLEDGMENTS

I'd like to acknowledge the people who helped me get me where I am today and gave me the strength to share my story. First and foremost, my mom, Diane, and my dad, Frank, for providing me with a foundation of love and support and the courage to chase a dream. To my beautiful children and family, who make me grateful each day and give me something to play for. To all the friends who stood by my side throughout when I was at my most vulnerable and always keep it real. To my high school basketball coach, NBA coaches, and coaches at all levels for all you've taught me about the game of life. To my teammates, who have been there with me during my best and worst. To AG, Mary, and my management team for being on this ride together all these years; to Dave for bringing this story to life; and Rick, Matthew, Brad, the team at Harmony Books in the United States and HarperCollins in Canada, and everyone who helped make this project happen. They called me "The Blessed One," and knowing the impact, big or small, that sharing my story can make on somebody, it really does make me feel blessed. Thank you all.

ABOUT THE AUTHOR

DEMAR DEROZAN is a guard/forward for the Chicago Bulls and has previously played for the San Antonio Spurs, Toronto Raptors, and USC Trojans. He is a two-time gold medalist for the United States basketball team. A father of five, DeRozan frequently returns to the gymnasiums and community centers in Compton, California, where he once practiced as a teenager, to mentor the next generation of basketball players.

ABOUT THE TYPE

This book was set in Caledonia, a typeface designed in 1939 by W. A. Dwiggins (1880–1956) for the Merganthaler Linotype Company. Its name is the ancient Roman term for Scotland, because the face was intended to have a Scottish-Roman flavor. Caledonia is considered to be a well-proportioned, businesslike face with little contrast between its thick and thin lines.

It's OK to not be OK.
If you are somebody who is seeking help,
there are resources available.
Call or text 9-8-8 or visit 988.ca (Canada)
or 988lifeline.org.